G000298284

Talking to the

Man of letters, man of faith, Su
all three.

Times Literary Supplement

Contained within the author's versatile voice there's an elegant and erudite conversation – passing on comments from literary giants or village gossips – which is also profoundly egalitarian . . . He talks simply and straightforwardly about great, grave and glorious things.

Here the poetry always present in any Blythe work . . . is perfectly complemented by illustrations from the lyrical East Anglian painter Mary Newcomb.

Eastern Daily Press

Blythe has a remarkable way of living, as it were, metaphorically, connecting and thus enriching everything – present and past, simple and complex, local and far-flung. Hard to say briefly how deeply satisfying this is.

The Oldie

Full of wisdom, country life, poetry, theology, expressed in an elegant economy of words.

The Door

Warmly recommended.

Church of England Newspaper

MARION GISSING
41 RIVERWAY COURT
RECORDER ROAD
NORWICH NR1 1BP

BY THE SAME AUTHOR

A Treasonable Growth
Immediate Possession
The Age of Illusion
William Hazlitt: Selected Writings
Akenfield
The View in Winter
Writing in a War
From the Headlands
The Short Stories of Ronald Blythe
Divine Landscapes
Private Words
Aldeburgh Anthology
Word from Wormingford
Going to Meet George
Talking about John Clare
First Friends
Out of the Valley
The Circling Year

TALKING TO THE NEIGHBOURS

*Conversations
from a Country Parish*

RONALD BLYTHE

Illustrations by
MARY NEWCOMB

CANTERBURY
PRESS
Norwich

© Ronald Blythe 2002
Illustrations © 2002 Mary Newcomb

First published in 2002 by the Canterbury Press Norwich
(a publishing imprint of Hymns Ancient & Modern Limited,
a registered charity)
St Mary's Works, St Mary's Plain,
Norwich, Norfolk, NR3 3BH

This paperback edition published 2003

www.scm-canterburypress.co.uk

All rights reserved. No part of this publication may be
reproduced, stored in a retrieval system, or transmitted,
in any form or by any means, electronic, mechanical,
photocopying or otherwise, without the prior permission
of the publisher, Canterbury Press.

The Author has asserted his right under the
Copyright, Design and Patents Act, 1988, to be
identified as the Author of this Work

British Library Cataloguing in Publication Data

A catalogue record for this book is available
from the British Library

ISBN 1−85311−553−3

Typeset by Rowland Phototypesetting Ltd,
Bury St Edmunds, Suffolk
Printed and bound in Great Britain by
Biddles Ltd, *www.biddles.co.uk*

CONTENTS

For Edward Storey

PREFACE

I have for many years now walked up from my somewhat isolated house to take Matins and Evensong in the linked parish churches of Wormingford, Mount Bures and Little Horkesley. These places grew up in the cleared woodland of the Suffolk–Essex border. They are untypically hilly, causing my old friend the artist John Nash, who painted them for decades, to dub them 'the Suffolk–Essex Highlands'. My Sunday duties have proved to be a personally fulfilling way for a poet and storyteller to remain close to those he has known for most of his life. Because it is not only certain farms which, due to their geography, have existed outside the general activity of the village, but certain kinds of people. The writer is both part of, yet separated from, society – a kind of odd man or woman out. Having my weekly church duties, I find, has a way of returning me to an historic centre whose both spiritual and social language is supportive, not to say at times fascinating.

The three churches, two ancient, one new – well 1958, built to replace the medieval one which vanished in a second in 1940 during a bombing raid – have varying degrees of churchmanship which only a born Anglican can understand, so best forget them and say one's prayers, sing, stare around, greet friends, listen to the ringers. They are kind enough to hear the same address, which is a combination of liturgy, natural and local history, poetry and diary. One of the functions of a writer is to be an interpreter and these addresses are an interpretation of my own world, which includes of course my faith. The subjects, like those in Scripture and liturgy, criss-cross one another. The length of the address is strictly ten minutes, else, as everyone knows, the tower will fall down. Often in my ear as I speak I catch the voice of someone on the Incumbents' Board, someone who spoke from where I am standing in 1350 or 1750, but alas I cannot hear what he is actually saying. Just a voice for his time.

MARY NEWCOMB

Artists and writers swiftly recognize a shared vision. It is not that they think or see things the same way, but that they find themselves capturing in their work certain minutiae and essentials which do not appear elsewhere. They possess a shared eye but a different medium. Mary Newcomb and myself are East Anglian contemporaries, she on the Suffolk–Norfolk border, myself on the Suffolk–Essex

Sidecar between banks of convolvulus

border. The light-drenched buildings, the glimpses of the locals in the lanes and the busy-ness of nature runs between us. I could ask for no greater compliment than her pleasure in giving me permission to have her work reproduced for *Talking to the Neighbours*. Those who want to know her work more should read *Mary Newcomb* by Christopher Andreae, published by Lund Humphries (1996), a collection of her paintings, plus extracts from her delightful diary.

R.B.

The Fields of Advent

———◆———

Quite suddenly, as always, we are close to Advent but the lesson is closer to harvest festival. So why are we hearing the Parable of the Sower? It is because a message like none other is being seeded to the world. Some of it won't be heard at all, fractions of it will be caught briefly but not retained, important bits of it will be held and then snatched from the recipient, and the whole of it will be caught and comprehended by a few. These catchers of the Word will act upon it.

These days we see Advent as a busy overture to Christmas and the economy sees it as a barometer for testing the nation's state of health. But the Church has always seen it with no small dread. It is not a comforting prospect for the world to have God as man in it. A God who calls himself the Word. Words have to be heard. It is their purpose.

Jesus, with his great experience of public speaking, knew all too well what usually happened when he addressed the message-hungry crowds which followed him about. How there were hard of hearing ears, truculent ears, eager ears, understanding ears, and ignorant ears which failed to make head or tail of what he was saying. Even his closest friends would sometimes protest that his meaning was obscure. All this, 'I will be with you' and 'I will not be with you' – promises like that. 'We do *not* follow you, Lord. Speak plainly.'

His parables were a kind of plain speaking. They are one of the most distinctive features of his ministry. There are the famous parables which we all know and which are among the world's most familiar short stories, and there are some semi-hidden parables here and there in the four Gospels which we probably miss. All in all it is thought that there are between thirty and forty parables in the teachings of Jesus. Most of them are set in the countryside and are examples of right and wrong responses to quite ordinary human dilemmas. They would have been like the moralizing tales told by the hearth or in the synagogue, except that they contained a further dimension, a dimension which was unsettling and haunting. These parables were not allegories, like *The Pilgrim's Progress*, because in an allegory every sentence can have a double meaning. A parable contains a single meaning and all its words lead up to this meaning.

The meaning, of course, of our hearing the Parable of the Sower in the days leading up to Advent is that the casting of the Word on the fertile and unfertile fields of the world has to begin. It is the inevitability of what is about to happen which causes the Church to catch its breath. The unavoidable-ness of Christ. Today's pre-Advent parable is so important that we find it in Matthew, Mark and Luke, and set out plainly at that. It was preached from a moored boat. Voices carry best across water and there was a huge crowd. Here was the most basic land lesson being taught by the sea. Here was the speaker's favourite analogy of our ears and wheat ears. 'Blessed are your ears, for they hear!' What they heard, as he sat on the ship and they stood on the shore, was about the most commonplace thing they knew. How broadcast seed went all over the place and was a dreadful waste, but show us the man who could put in his corn and not lose half of it and you will be showing us a miracle! In springtime – not approaching dead of winter – you went out to the field, the new seed in a bag tied to your belt, and you cast it right then left, striding up and down, and from middle to edge, and you sang, 'One for me, one for the birds!' It could not be helped if quite a lot fell where it could not germinate or if weeds smothered it. This was farming for you. You had to be satisfied with being able to take out only a fraction of what you put into it. Thus it had always been.

Christ had to throw his voice. How else could it have reached those crowds? 'Blessed are your ears – for they hear!' There must have been many who only just caught his words but all would have recognized a master-storyteller. Story-telling was as ordinary an occupation in first-century Palestine as sowing seed. But unlike some of the parables, this one stresses the commonplace, the thing which everybody knows. Those who like stories like them to transcend the matter-of-fact, else why tell them? But ordinary activities have to be re-seen. They require vision as much as does some remarkable idea or plan. Christ is teaching his listeners how to harvest his words.

There were two grain harvests at the time of the Lord's ministry, one of barley, one of wheat. Two sowings, two reapings. And in a stony land which alternated between hot and cold, and which was lively with hungry birds. The agricultural scene could not have been more unlike our ruled fields with not a blade out of line and not a weed in sight. And all as level as a board, and not a yard of them applicable to the parable whose imagery suggests an inefficient farming rather than a helpless human condition. You gained some, you lost some. It could be a cornstalk, it could be a child. It could be words. Time and time again the great teacher called his class to order – 'You who have ears to hear – let him hear!' He must be heard in depth, not shallowly. His words will be attacked. Corn-seed being throttled by thistles was again a common sight. 'You', he tells the crowd, 'are my field and you are also my labourers and farmers – are you listening?' He quotes the prophet Isaiah who now and then threw up his hands in despair at thick-headedness – 'You will hear all right but you won't understand, you will see but without perception.' 'Do not be hard of hearing,' Christ implores us during Advent.

But there are things which we do not want to hear at this time. Christmas bells, yes. The first cries of the Bethlehem child, yes. His mother's song of joy, yes. But not all this worrying talk of a second entry into our world. The infant in the straw, yes. The Christ in judgement, no. Let *him* be art. An Advent Gospel has the Pharisees – 'the separated ones' – and the orthodox Jews coming together to plan, in the words of St Matthew, 'how they might entangle him in his talk'. How about if they trip him up with the old question about loyalty to Rome? 'Master, we know you are true and teach a true way to God, and that you pay little attention to criticism, so be straight with us. Is it legal or right that we should pay tax to Caesar?' They meant as well as the tax which they had to pay to the Temple. Was it right that their poor little country should contribute to the empire? 'Show me the tribute money,' he tells them. 'And whose head is on it?' 'Why, Caesar's.' 'Then give to Caesar what belongs to him, and give to God what is his alone.'

Advent approaches and the days darken. The manger is not prepared. A fortune begins to change hands in the high street. Many shining things – and to be honest, many generous actions – distract our proper attention from the enormous reality of God's human birth, for which we are thankful. Let this too become an especially beautiful parable and something we can cope with. 'Very well,' says the child, 'I will teach you in tales, in homely country moralities such as you like to hear. But take care, let no grain of my teaching, not a stray word fail to take root for one reason or another. Let us together be sowers and reapers, hearers and doers, green then golden, harvesters and harvested.'

Except Thou Bless Me

A t the close of the service comes the blessing. The priest says 'I' and I say 'we'. He gives what is known as the authoritative blessing but I include myself in a blessing. The priest is giving the congregation the official blessing of the Church but I am giving a blessing in all our names. But whether authoritative or collective, blessing is blessing. We say 'God bless you' at the end of a letter and at a child's bedside as we put the light out. And now and then, having listened to some personal disaster or anxiety we murmur these three words as sincerely as we are able.

In the sixty-seventh Psalm, the *Deus Misereatur*, which begins with our pleading to God to bless us and ends with our being confident that he will, there is a central burst of happiness, of realization that life itself springs from blessing. Because 'God, even our own God', is giving it to us. What does it mean, this religious thing we call 'blessing'? It means to confer what we ourselves have experienced of God's care on another being. Blessedness has to be something which can be passed on. St Thomas Aquinas described perfect blessedness as a vision of God, in which case, when we bless a friend, we could be passing on our own understanding of who God is, the giver of everything which has contributed to our better nature, as it were.

It is easy to bless those we love or even those we manage to get along with, or the wide muddled world at large. So easy in fact that Christ obliges each one of us, and not just the praying Church, to go far beyond such natural good wishes towards our relations and neighbours, to go beyond our circle, and certainly beyond the impersonally circling world. 'Bless them that curse you!' To do this can be the most devastating response to the cruel, the ignorant, the intolerant, the malicious, the jealous. It can leave them without a leg to stand on. Although it was not intended as such, a blessing of those who hate can be the best psychology. What Jesus meant when he told us to bless those who hate us was to extend the power of love to where it is most denied. To bless undermines evil. Jesus's unorthodox blessings undermined so many of the conventionally held religious and social attitudes of his day that those listening to him must have felt their world falling apart. But blessed indeed was that shaking out of prejudice, that challenging of conventional morality.

Alexander Pope, writing to a friend, said, 'Blessed is the man who expects nothing, for he shall never be disappointed' was the ninth beatitude. Many of us expect more than life can give where we are concerned. Hopes run high when we are young but gradually as the years mount up, although the big thing we expected has not come our way, a number of smaller things which amount to a sizeable gift have. Common sense as well as courtesy towards God make us recognize them as blessings. One could be plain good health. One which is taken for granted is freedom. We now have a window on the world in our sitting-rooms through which nightly we are shown illness, lack of freedom and such an absence of blessedness as to make us wonder where the blessed Lord is. He is, of course, in the pain, in the struggle. Those who we see suffering will be blessing him – though, 'What for?', we could be asking. Looking through our nightly window on the world we also see the tremendous fuss we make over some usually brief inconvenience, often to do with the weather. Some supply is threatened and there on our screens is the rush to the supermarkets as though Hitler was about to invade. Scenes of Third World privation touch our hearts and bring a guilty feeling to our blessedness. At the same time we see in some starved or violent land a face radiant with blessing. That of an old man or a mother, or a boy laughing, or a child in the sun. How and why this should be we cannot tell, but there he or she is, radiating the blessed image of God in the midst of poverty or war. 'Through such souls alone,' wrote Robert Browning, 'God stooping shows sufficient of His Light for us in the dark to rise by.'

It can come to us in the West as a bit of a shock to recognize that it is we who could be in the dark and who need some blessed illumination from those who have nothing else to give. All that they possess is – light! We can only give what we have, and those that have little give most. This is the nub of the widow's mite.

Jesus devoted part of his Sermon on the Mount to states of blessedness. He covers every aspect of how we might qualify for it. If we know that we have a need of God we are blessed, if we are sorrowful or gentle or fighters for justice or merciful or pure in heart or peacemakers or suffer persecution and insults for our love of God, we are blessed. Each one of us at some time or other has both deserved and received God's blessing during a time of need or a time of courage, or maybe just a time of common sense. Jesus was in the actual act of blessing when he left this earth, and many people have done likewise, blessed those they loved with their last breath, especially their children. 'Count your blessings', says the old hymn, 'name them one by one'. And indeed we should – and so we do. We add them to those huge blessings in the Lord's sermon. Blessings change with the years. The blessings of youth are unlikely to be the same as those of old age. We move from blessedness to blessedness.

One of the reasons why we come to this ancient building week after week is to stock ourselves up with blessings. I shall soon say, 'And the blessing of God Almighty, the Father, the Son, and the Holy Spirit, be amongst us, and remain with us always' and certain old friends will bless me at the door as they put their books away and find their car keys. Portia's mercy, you may recall, was *twice* blessed because it blessed the giver and the receiver. But *all* blessing possesses this quality. When we bless someone, we are blessed in return.

We could find ourselves hard put to explain exactly why we come to church regularly. Although I had not asked her such a question, someone gave me her answer – 'If I miss my service the whole week is different – not right. It is a blessing to be here.' Long ago St Paul, and Timothy his young assistant, wrote a letter to the Christians at Corinth which began by reminding them of God's consolation. 'He comforts us in all our troubles, so that we in turn may be able to comfort others in any trouble of theirs and to share with them the consolation we ourselves receive from God' (2 Cor. 1.4 NEB). Similarly with blessing. We live within a cycle of blessedness. There are times when we feel it in the air or see it in a stranger's glance. We hear it being put into a beautiful language at the Eucharist or Evensong. Paul's second letter to the Corinthians reminds them that they are all in the same boat, he, Timothy, the new little church down by the harbour, all the city, all humanity. And thus it is a universal blessedness which encompasses both himself and them. And so he ends his letter as he usually does, 'Be perfect, be of good comfort, be of one mind, live in peace ... Greet one another with a holy kiss.'

Here is Robert Browning again:

> That what began best can't end worst,
> Nor what God blessed once, prove accursed.

These lines are from a poem called 'Apparent Failure'.

Being Born

These past December days have been noisy with babies, keen to show off their helplessness, Alice, Jacob and Zachary included. The old masters would now and then show the new-born Christ-child sitting up and already ruling the world. None to my knowledge showed him crying. There he is, flat on his mother's lap, or in the golden straw, taking his first wandering stare at those looking down on him. To understand the divinity of Jesus we have first to see the naturalness of Jesus.

Much has been said of the lowliness of this birth, the makeshift arrival in the inn's stable and not in its best bedroom, forgetting what the latter would have been like at tax time. Much better where the sweet-breathed animals settled down for the night. For centuries children in that country and our own were born on fresh straw and then, washed and wrapped, taken into their parents' bed. This was how it was done. The simplicity of Christ's birth was most beautiful and most ordinary. It happened in winter when humanity and animals huddled close, when they shared small space – when they shared everything, in fact, shelter, toil, warmth and the land outside. It is the tenderness of the Lord's birth, matching as it does the tenderness of our birth, which moves us. Glimpsing it in Gospel or gallery, there rushes into our heads and hearts our concern for his survival. Coming into the world is such a hazard. We may have waved our own magic around him, as we do our own babies, and out of our love for him, but the look he gives us from text or frame is one of huge reality. The Creator has entered his creation, that is the truth of the matter. This is why rustics and intellectuals both fell to their knees. This is why bad rulers shook in their shoes. This is why the angels sang. This is why the animals felt so much at home.

I don't doubt that all this week the clergy have been racking their heads for something fresh to say at the 'Midnight', but one can hardly be original about the birth of Christ, although poets and shopkeepers can surprise us now and then. And so, here we all are once again, the tree switched on, the toy crib by the pulpit, fluttering candles everywhere, cars huddling near the graves, but not with the snow on snow which the weatherman promised. So let us take the birthday story back to its origins, that told us by Matthew and Luke. Mark does not tell it – the child has become the man in Mark. John deals with it as breathtaking metaphor, as Word made flesh which 'dwelt among us – and we beheld his glory, the glory of the only begotten of the Father, full of grace and truth'. And so we approach the Christmas altar, careful not to ignite the chancel holly, suddenly finding 'adoring' the only thing to do. This service grew out of the need of Christ's friends to be among the first at the stable on his birthday. We bring to it our best selves, our imagination, our practicality and of course our wonder. Where would we be without wonder? We allow ourselves a big helping of happiness. Communion.

Christmas finds the journalism of misery and inconvenience in full spate. Shopping is torture, travel is hell. But my old friend flying from Berlin to Bottengoms arrives quite joyfully. It is Friday evening and he says the Kiddush, coming as he does from the same race as the child. We stand around the already laid dinner table with various hats on our heads. We light seven candles, we eat all the broken bread and sip wine. The young guest then reads a psalm in Hebrew and translates the Sabbath eve prayers, and I think, as I always do, here is both Last Supper and First Eucharist. I also think, as I always do, that if only folk of all faiths would sometimes share each other's sacraments, why, what a different world it would be!

Joachim – this Christmas guest – is a garden architect. His last job was to redesign the main Jewish cemetery in Berlin. He has created several acres of park with paths like a star, juniper trees and a synagogue chapel. No potter's field this. As yet there is not a single grave. At the dedication ceremony everyone had to walk round it seven times. It took all day! A high iron fence has had to be set up to keep the Nazi yobbos out. For it is not only the poor who are always with us, but the cruel, the ignorant, the evil. Maybe you listened to Bishop Richard Holloway's condemnation of such people when he spoke on the radio about what Bethlehem really means in these times. There was none of the usual condemnation of the West's buying spree at this period. He, like me, had strolled through the Christmas streets of a great city and had been overwhelmed by the inherent goodness and beauty of humanity at large. He saw its beautiful ordinariness and its kindness, its privacy and its mystery. Also its mixture of eloquence and incoherence where religion was concerned. But of one thing the bishop was certain, that God loved these people, and that they unconsciously imaged his love.

And so on this his latest birthday we crowd in the ancient midnight church to see the boy born to be king. 'God, who at sundry times and in divers manners spake in times past unto our fathers via the prophets, has in these last days spoken unto us.' Emmanuel! God with us – at last! God on earth. We look at him and recognize that his and our lives now turn in a cycle of blessedness. The Christmas hymns and the liturgy of the Christmas Mass put this blessedness in a lucid language which will hum around in our heads for days to come. Seeing the brightness of his glory for the first time, and conquering their fear, the friends of Jesus said, 'It is good, Lord, to be here!' And so it is for us, good to kneel where generations have knelt before, to take part yet again in the ceremony of birth and love and gifts and gratitude. The poet Emily Dickinson thought back to its origins:

Being Born

What Inn is this
Where for the night
Peculiar Traveller comes?
Who is the Landlord?
Where the maids?
Behold, what curious rooms!
No ruddy fires on the hearth –
No brimming Tankards flow –
Necromancer! Landlord!
Who are these below?

Consequences

————◆————

The first Christians believed that their Lord would return next week, next month, next year. Very soon anyway. But here is the third millennium and still he has not come. Yet Advent implores us to be awake, to be watchful. 'Know ye that the kingdom of God is at hand . . . they shall see the Son of Man coming in a cloud with power and great glory. And when these things begin to come to pass, then look up, and lift up your heads, for your redemption draweth nigh.' (Luke 21.31, 27–28 KJV)

This is Christ in majesty. This is Advent's huge and less welcome statement. Far easier is the counting off the days for the birth of Christ in the manger. Throughout the centuries the second coming has created far more unease than welcome. There were times when it was taken literally and times when it was taken symbolically, and now there are times like our own when we do not know how to take it and put it on hold, so to speak. All that we can admit as yet one more Advent approaches is that we should indeed stir up our seriousness, for without a doubt it is an immense happening which lies ahead of us.

Why did Herod move swiftly in an attempt to stamp out this birth? To nip it in the bud? It was because he saw its consequences, perhaps not only for his own little kingdom but for kings everywhere. Birth has to end in death anyway, so why not shorten the process in this instance and save the world a lot of worry? It was one of those radical having to be cruel to be kind acts, his infanticide. One has to pay a high price sometimes to keep the peace. Children are being slaughtered in Bethlehem as I write. When was it ever any different? Herod's mistake was in not realizing that this birth could not be destroyed by death, it being the incarnation of love. It is because of it that each of us continues to journey, not in the direction of the grave, but to God. During Advent we think of his journey to us and ours to him, and we prepare for the meeting. This must be both awe-full – and cheerful. We are glad and happy, and uneasy and frightened all at the same time. The music of the angels and the music of the tills accompanies us.

One of the consequences of God arriving in our earthly situation, which is what he is about to do, is that we will have to stand before him and confess our inhumanity. Advent is not an easy time. We shall need all our strength to cope with its implications. One of the stories for its approach is that of the feeding of the five thousand, which at first glance looks an odd tale to be told on the final Sunday of the Church's year. Jesus had been busy as usual, breaking the Sabbath to heal the sick and saying things like, 'My Father never ceased his work, so I must work too', even on the Sabbath. And adding, 'A time is coming when the spiritually dead shall hear his voice and will come to life!' This is the preface to the feeding of the five thousand. Jesus is stirring up those who have accompanied him on the long march which was his ministry, nourishing them, awakening them to the fulfilled life, not a half-life. 'Wake up, for the Master draws nigh.' What, this child our Master? But babies grow up, with huge consequences for all in their sphere.

We shall most come to life in Advent hymns which place our dread and delight side by side in words and tunes which help to rationalize – or poeticize – a theology we find hard to bear. That 'Wake, O wake! with tidings thrilling', for example, in which neither child nor judge is due, but a bridegroom for lovers such as us. As the four Sundays proceed, so does their solemnity. Nothing is to be taken lightly. God is near. Realizing how terrifying this could be for us, Jesus tells us a story about a bad lot son and a forgiving father. Here it is the son who approaches and the father who waits. A father who, like so many parents whose children have led them a dance and left them for years without so much as a letter or telephone call, has been ever on the look out for a familiar figure, his thoughts of reconciliation, not of blame. This father sees a hungry, ragged young man staggering home, and so terrified of what he expects to hear that he has rehearsed a grovelling speech. 'Disown me as a son – make me a servant. It is all I deserve.' The worst thing is that he cannot forget his father's kindness and understanding that young men have a right to their mistakes, for this son had been given his share of the family money when he asked for it. Nothing had been put in his way when he said that he was off to the big city. It was, 'Take it, it was yours from the beginning for you to do what you like with it.'

The son expected his father's wrath but would he have come home had he expected his father's rejection? We sense that he would not. He would have stood the consequences of his wasted life, would have descended to vagrancy, sickness and early death. We see boys and girls in cardboard boxes in shop doorways. What parents stare through windows for a glimpse of them? What love was ever shown them? What an adventure it was when these sons and daughters ran off to the city lights! The Lord's tale is one of the oldest tales, yet the most haunting. It says everything which can be said about our returning to our Father's ways after doing what we liked. 'Love is not love which alters when it alteration finds' wrote Shakespeare. The prodigal was a sorry sight, hardly recognizable as the person who had left home, full of high hopes, well-dressed, confident. But he cannot be disowned or disinherited, for he is the father's *son*.

It is the Father's Son whom we inherit at Bethlehem. No best robe, no ring, no banquet, but some telling presents from those who know what will happen to him anon, and some shepherds' songs. An unknown author once wrote about 'the blending of dread and love' in a book called *The Cloud of Unknowing*. The blending of dread and love is what Advent is. It is a time for deep, deep reverence. The soon to be born Christ is waiting for the natural moment to become part of nature, and we wait with him. We wait too for someone less understandable to us, King Jesus in judgement.

> Ye servants of the Lord
> Each for your Master wait,
> Observant of his heavenly word,
> And watchful at his gate.

Epiphanies

———◆———

1

W hen we open a door, a box, ourselves, what is inside
becomes manifest. Something which was hidden
shows itself. For centuries before Christ the prophets had
spoken of a spiritual force which remained hidden like a
seed in humanity, but which one day must burst forth and
show itself as part of the purpose of God. He himself would
be manifest in a new-born child, in a precocious boy in the
Temple, in a poor homeless adult wandering the dusty
roads, in a welcome guest at Bethany, in a great teacher
who would sometimes pause to become a great doctor, in
a figure of fun in the charge-room of a court, in an executed
felon. Epiphany.

I was listening to someone making an interesting point
about the three wise men, how they had gradually changed
from being wise men to being magi and from magi to kings
– King Gaspar, King Melchior and King Balthasar, three
monarchs you will not find in Scripture. And why these
grand people have become so important in the humble
Christmas story, and why they dominate the Epiphany. The
point was this. That so strong was the emphasis of Christ's

own kingdom being for the poor and simple, that anyone who was rich or clever might feel that they were excluded from it. I have always felt sympathy for that well-off young man who was told that he would need to offload all his possessions if he wanted to get to heaven. But even this was easier to do than to hold rather elementary notions about this life and the next if one happens to be intellectual. Thus the reason why the Magi – one black, of course – came to hold such an important position was because they showed (epiphany) how it really does take all sorts to populate the kingdom of God. The rich and the clever certainly have more power and opportunity to do harm, but they *can* be holy! And poor and ignorant folk cannot enter the kingdom on this account alone. They too have to show the Christ within them.

We may think that we progress, but we do not change much. Was there anything done in Jesus's day more dreadful than what is done in ours? More cruel? More unfair? More vain? Greedier? Was his healing ministry ever more needed? His touch? His intimacy? 'Ephphatha', we hear him command, maybe wearily, for we are as closed up as ever. 'Be open!' He talks to us all through history. 'Be open to one another, no matter who or what you are. Are you not all dwellers in my kingdom? I have manifested myself to you, the dull, the bright, the hurt, the lucky ones. It is Epiphany. I show you myself.' In his famous poem 'The Journey of the Magi', T. S. Eliot made these brilliant travellers say:

We returned to our places, these Kingdoms,
But no longer at ease here, in the old dispensation.

2

How long, how many years, those two old people, Simeon
and Anna, had been scanning that seemingly endless procession of parents climbing the Temple steps to present
their baby sons to God we have no idea. It was the custom
for mothers to be ritually purified by the rabbi after giving
birth, and for their sons to be numbered for the state.
Simeon had been assured that he would see the Messiah
before he died. And thus he would have watched as the
babes in arms were carried by. Was this he? Surely this
angelic little boy must be what the prophet called 'the consolation of Israel'? All the children would have looked
heavenly as they slept. Anna, the old lady, she was eighty-
four and a widow, also watched. She was a familiar figure
at the Temple, always there, always at prayer, a kind of
hermit. How would the one for whom they had waited so
long 'manifest' himself? For this is what Epiphany means
– manifestation. To be manifest is to be perceived. Thus
the old couple had no worries on this score. When the
Christ arrived, even if his parents were common folk and
he himself an ordinary-looking child, they would know –
instantly! They did not have to look for strange signs.

As it happened, the story so beautifully told by Luke, the
Holy Spirit gave Simeon and Anna a nudge – 'This is the

one.' All the great religions are based on enlightenment. Without them, and in spite of the darkness which they occasionally engender at times, the world would be a black place. I have been reading about the Buddha, that enlightened teacher whose religion has done less harm in the world than all the others. The great Buddhist leaders such as the Dalai Lama are recognized in infancy, just as Jesus was by Simeon and Anna. The present Dalai Lama was an apparently ordinary little boy but those who were searching for the child into whom they believed the spirit of the last sacred leader had passed were in no doubt that it now lived in him. And we, who know so little about Buddhism, seeing the present Dalai Lama on our television screens, can have no doubt that he was the right choice. For here, manifest in this smiling person, is love, wisdom, courage and holiness.

The Buddha himself was one of humanity's most sublime teachers, and for centuries before Christ. Like Jesus, he never wrote a book and all that we know of him, again like Jesus, is contained in the stories and sayings collected by those who saw him and listened to him. His title 'Buddha' means enlightened, or awakened. He was born in the foothills of Nepal into a princely family. He was much loved and kept in a state of artificial innocence, growing up with no knowledge of the world which lay outside his palace and its lovely grounds. He was in his twenties when curiosity overcame him about his kingdom and one day he ordered his coachman to drive him through the magnificent gates and into the countryside. They passed an old man bent double.

'Who is that?'

'He is what they call an old man, my Lord, because he has not long to live.'

'Shall I become an old man then?'

'Yes, my Lord. We are all of a kind to grow old.'

'Then enough of this outside world today. Drive me back.'

And in his exquisite room the young prince told himself, 'Shame be upon this thing called birth, since it means growing old.'

A few days later, driving abroad, he saw a sick man lying on the ground having his dressings done.

'That man, what has he done, for his eyes and his voice are not like ours?'

'He is what is called ill, my Lord.'

'Shall I become ill?'

'Yes, my Lord, we all fall ill.'

Back in his room, the prince said, 'Shame on this thing called birth, since it leads to decay and disease for all of us.'

Soon, once more driving far from his palace, he saw a shaven-headed man, a wanderer, clothed in a simple yellow robe.

'What has that man done – his head and clothes are not like ours?'

'He is what is called a wanderer, my Lord, *one who has gone forth.*'

'What is that – to have gone forth?'

'It means to lead a holy life, my Lord, one which is filled only with good actions, good conduct, harmlessness and kindness.'

The Buddha alighted. 'Take my carriage back. I will cut off my hair, don a yellow robe and go forth.'

Which, after he had upset the Nazareth synagogue, is what Jesus did. Both he and the Buddha, and countless of their followers, went forth, carrying light with them.

Epiphany is when we see everything plainly, when we recognise God plainly, when we walk in the light. When we follow a star, which means having to look up. It is a realistic journey during which we see the world for what it is, a hard place. A natural place where we are mortal and so will have difficulties and infirmities. But light accompanies us and we are able to see further than our hurts.

The Epistle tells us of gifts. Three clever men followed the light of a star to give a child presents which would symbolize his fate. St Paul, writing to his fellow Romans, has a gift-list made out by God. Whatever he gives us, says Paul, we must accept it with humility and then *use it*. Perhaps ministry has been handed out to us, or teaching, or the gift to love others. Brotherly love, maybe, which means a natural love for our neighbours. He recommends affection, patience and hospitality, and being of what he calls 'the same mind'. 'Show yourselves in the best light,' he tells us.

> Lo, sages from the east are gone
> To where the star hath newly shone:
> Led on by light to Light they press
> And by their gifts their God confess.

This poem was written for an Epiphany in the fifth century.

3

There is a second child in the Epiphany story, which is why it used to celebrate the first child's baptism, only when he was grown up. That Jesus should accept baptism shocked his cousin John. John was preaching national renewal down by the river, the washing away the soiled society, the rising out of the water a cleansed people. And there strides towards him the Christ. Soon he is in his arms and is taken under, although there is nothing to wash away. All three evangelists record it, how Jesus came to hear what John was saying – to hear his own herald – and to be like other men although he was God.

The Jews liked to know their own history. Their national and personal past was most familiar to them. How special they felt! But how hard it was to live up to, this chosenness. Their preoccupation with history made it impossible for them to be free of it, and in fact what they knew about themselves both uplifted them – and dragged them down. Whilst always acknowledging the great men in Jewish history, and reminding his countrymen of how they had sometimes been treated, Jesus would now and then show a harsh irreverence towards old customs, old ways of constantly looking back. 'Let the dead bury their dead.' 'Give us this *day* our *daily* bread.' Christ is the teacher of daily-ness, of finding nourishment in the present.

When St Paul took Christianity out into the non-Jewish world he often found people who had no knowledge of their ancestors. Jews were most careful to know their family trees. All those 'begats'. Although the Lord's own family tree was meticulously placed at the beginning of the Gospels, he was indifferent to it. 'Who is my mother?' 'Who are my brothers?' He was, as John said, Word made flesh, Light which was our life. Someone who possessed human ancestry, someone who was beyond it.

The authorities could not see what was so clearly manifest in John the Baptist. They sent a deputation to question him. 'Who are you? Are *you* the Christ? Are you Elijah, or Elisha, perhaps?' Instead of answering, 'I am John the son of Zechariah', the strangely dressed young man replied that he was a voice crying in the wilderness, 'Make straight the way of the Lord!' 'Who gave you permission to baptize?' demanded the delegation. It was then that John pointed to Jesus, who was approaching, and said, 'There, standing among you, is someone you do not recognize. Someone whose shoes I am not fit to remove.'

It is a tremendous moment, the presence of Jesus in a crowd waiting for renewal, a queue of men and women longing to be seen in a better light. They would have removed their clothes and sandals at the river's edge, and Christ would have done the same. The naked Word steps forward to John like everyone else and asks for baptism. Poor John is aghast. 'It is you who should baptize me!' Coming out of the water, Jesus did what everyone else did, he knelt in prayer. His father acknowledges him – 'You are my beloved son.'

Raindrops after frost

An Epiphany reading from Romans has Paul urging us 'to be transformed by the renewing of our minds'. Everyone seeking baptism in the Jordan knew what they had to do – be transformed. A new year, and the Epiphany, or showing of Christ to the world beyond Jerusalem, they arrive together. There are only a couple of New Year hymns, one which we used to sing when we returned to school after the Christmas holiday, 'Father, let me dedicate all this year to thee'. It is one of those impossible attempts at holiness.

Lawrence Tuttiet wrote it. He was a Victorian canon of St Ninian's Cathedral, Perth. Like so many hymns at that time, it is haunted by sickness and death and by an uncertainty about anything except God's ultimate protection. Perhaps it is significant that it comes from Scotland, where Hogmanay takes precedence over Christmas. The coming year begins to manifest itself in the January darkness. Natural light joins the light which Christ brings into the world. We begin to identify ourselves.

4

The child grows up during Epiphany. But his parents, as with most parents, go on seeing a child when he is a youth. When he has a mind of his own. Which is why the story of Jesus giving Mary and Joseph the slip during the great Passover Festival at Jerusalem is among the Epiphany readings. This family, like most Jewish families, had travelled a long way to take part in the annual thanksgiving, surrounded as it was with all the fun of the fair. There were pleasures and dangers, holiness and wildness all mixed up. Like Christmas with us, there was a sacred dimension and a party dimension. There were huge crowds and excitements. The Lord's family was part of a group travelling back to Nazareth and had assumed that he was jogging along, perhaps with the other young people, and they had gone a whole day's journey, perhaps twenty miles, when they found he was missing. He was just twelve years old, just the age to get kidnapped by slave-traders, maybe, or to get into trouble, or to be very frightened, or to be hurt by the world. So his parents trudged all the way to the Holy City once more which to them was no longer a delight but a nightmare. There they searched for three days – and we can imagine the kind of places which they would have gone to – for one does not look in fine gardens and restaurants for a poor child who is becoming a youth. We don't know why it never occurred to them to go to the Temple in the first place or why they went to it as a last resort. Did they go there in desperation to ask God to bring Jesus back to them safe and sound? Or did somebody say, 'A boy . . .'? And there would have followed a tearful description of what he looked like. What did he look like? None of the Gospels tells us. And then, 'Oh, he's in the Temple arguing with the teachers.' Luke, a doctor, writes simply, 'And it came to pass, that after three days they found him in the Temple, sitting in the midst of the doctors, both hearing them, and asking them questions. And all that heard him were astonished at his understanding and answers' (Luke 2.46–47).

It should be explained that argument and debate were a traditional activity in both the Temple and the synagogues, although children were not supposed to be heard in them. And it should also be explained that thirteen-year-old boys once went to Oxford and Cambridge, and that Romeo and Juliet were fourteen. Jesus's skill and precocity in debate must have intrigued the doctors, else they would have told him to run away. Who *was* he? His parents were asking themselves the same question. Having 'shown' who he was (epiphany) the growing boy went home – to grow up. It is one of the most human stories in the New Testament. We too sometimes need to search for Christ and not always to believe that he is conveniently at hand. There could be days, months, years even, when we won't see him, at least not as brightly as we once did, and we will be filled with loss and anxiety. And there will be times when we won't understand him. But if, as an Epiphany reading advises us, we 'renew our minds', then we shall catch him up and he will be close once more.

5

Some time ago I had to edit *The Penguin Book of Diaries* and, of course, ninety-nine out of a hundred began with a solemn awareness that a page had turned for ever in the life of the diarist. 'Call back yesterday, bid time return!' cries Lord Salisbury in Shakespeare's play *Richard II*. He and King Richard have missed their chance and want to have another go. But Time never returns, never stands still, does not move on without us. The diarist tells himself, 'I have a clean sheet on which nothing yet has been written. That is a comfort.' Generally speaking, a new year does not make us feel as old as a new birthday. On the contrary, its untried possibilities are likely to make us feel youthful and excited.

Poor Dr Johnson, who was better than most of us

could ever be, had dreadful New Years. January after January he wrote down resolutions which were beyond his capacity to keep, to get up early in the morning, to 'lose no time', and so on. 'I have now spent fifty years in resolving, having from the earliest times been forming schemes for a better life. I have done nothing', he wrote. This was not true. Although none of us should boast of our achievements, our kindnesses, etc., we should recognize them.

Here are some of Dr Johnson's New Year resolutions, put down when he was an old man – an old man who could not change his ways, and indeed did not have to:

To apply to study.
To rise early.
To go to church.
To drink less.
To oppose laziness.
To put my books in order.

He should have made another list which said, 'I have taken a poor blind woman into my house and cared for her. I have taken a black boy into my house, fed him, educated him and made him my son.' And this list could go on for many pages.

New Year is the time for admitting our merits as well as our failures. God in the form of a human being is with us. He is shown to us, and we need to show our true self to – ourself! Here am I in the image of God. Here am I on my time journey to him. And what pleasures I shall have on the way. Friendships, music, the countryside, love, food, quietness, travel, books, prayer, the garden – the list is endless.

During the Epiphany we ask God, who governs all things, to grant us his peace all the days of our life, to use what gifts he has given us, and to show what we are made of. Such openness has its danger. The Magi were open with Herod, being honest men, thus exposing the one they had come to seek to danger. After they had presented their gifts, the stable was in turmoil. They had to find their way home by a secret route and the child and his parents could not return home at all but had to take flight to Egypt. Something so manifestly tremendous for the world, the coming into it of its Creator, could not be hidden. The Light of the world was from the start a journeying light which some would have liked to snuff out. Our faith is not shut away, the preserve of the 'faithful' only. It is uncontainable. 'I have come to open blind eyes,' says Jesus, 'to bring out the prisoners from prison, and them that sit in darkness out of the prison house.' He means that he will release us from ourselves.

Christ would have known Isaiah's prophecy:

> I will bring the blind by a way that they knew not: I will lead them in paths that they have not known: I will make darkness light before them, and crooked things straight ... Hear, ye deaf, look, ye blind that ye may see! (Isa. 42.16, 18 KJV)

Man describing a half moon path

This morning, as I was getting ready for church, the winter sun broke through, filling the house with a light whose brilliance I had almost forgotten. Ordinary objects manifested a glory and the footpath to the farm over the hill became a pilgrim route.

The Lord's Economy

With Epiphany past, we begin to count the days to the resurrection, count the days to our redemption. Some of these days were once used as a preparation for the Lenten fast, but now we use them to celebrate the natural world. The readings are all about the creation of the universe, and also about a mysterious thing called 'the Word' which did not have to be created because it already existed. What 'Word'? Well a Greek word called Logos, or Reason. In the beginning was the Reason for us and our world. And then God so loved what he had created that he entered it and died for it. We are on difficult theological ground, yet, as we read the opening pages of Genesis and the first lines of St John's Gospel, these grand sentences, even if they cannot be fully explained, carry with them something which we are able to understand.

First, Genesis: 'In the beginning of Creation, when God made heaven and earth, the earth was without form and void, with darkness over the face of the abyss, and a mighty wind that swept over the waters. So God said, "Let there be light."'

And then St John: 'The Word was with God at the beginning, and nothing was created without him. All that came to be was *alive with his life*, and that life was the light of men.'

We listen to these profound statements as the days begin to lengthen and nature begins to stir. We notice a change in the atmosphere, a movement, a force. This year the spring is well ahead of itself, as we say. A mild winter has brought us masses of February flowers. A reading for this time is one of Jesus's workaday stories about vineyards. Palestine provided ideal conditions for growing grapes. They were used for making wine, the common drink, and for making raisins, the common food. The plants were set out in long rows, just as we see them in France and Italy to this day. With their single root and many winding branches, they made people think of their family trees. There was the original root in its native soil and buds shooting in all directions to mature and bear fruit.

Vineyards are work intensive. A number of people must manure, train and prune in the spring, and gather grapes in the autumn. The grapes must too be protected from birds and vermin, not to mention robbers. Extra hands have to be hired for harvesting the crop. The grape harvest was the last of the three annual harvests which formed the agricultural economy of the Middle East. For Christ the vineyard was an image of those who lived by God's law, who did his work, who carried out his orders and who, eventually, would be rewarded with his wages. It was also an image of the Christian family – 'I am the root, you are the branches' – and there were chilling references to the cutting out and burning of dead wood.

In Jesus's most stern vineyard story we are not told which busy time of the year it is, spring or autumn. But we do know that extra labour is wanted at once either to prune or pick. The owner of the vineyard goes to the hiring-place early in the morning and employs a number of workers at a penny a day. We saw this kind of thing in East Anglia not so very long ago. Extra hands for fruit-picking and pea-picking – piece-work it was called. So much a bag or a skip. The workers agreed to it before they started. One of the important things which we have to remember about the parables is their social reality. Jesus is telling stories about rural matters which those who heard them would know all about. His workers agreed to labour for a penny a day. We don't know the going rate but we can be sure that he did. Had he said sixpence a day his audience would not have stayed to listen to the rest of the tale. 'What did he know about running a vineyard?'

When it came to wages, Christ always knew what he was talking about. He once told some soldiers, 'No bullying, no blackmail, make do with your pay.' And so the vineyard man goes to the hiring place at dawn and picks out some good workers. But soon, realizing that he is understaffed, he returns to hire a few more – at a penny a day. And so on until the evening, and always at a penny a day. To the last group he says,

'Why do you stand here idle all the day?'

'Because no one has hired us, sir.'

'Then go you also into the vineyard and whatsoever is right, so you will receive.'

The night comes, when no man should work. The owner orders his steward to pay the workers their wages 'beginning with the last to be hired and then going back to the first. Give them each a penny.' Well, you don't have to be a trade unionist to know what would happen. There was uproar. Those who had been there since dawn shouted, 'Some of these men have only worked one hour – and have been paid a penny! Surely we who have toiled for many hours and have borne the burden and heat of the day should have more money.'

But the vineyard owner reminds the protesters of something they had forgotten. The agreement struck at the hiring-place. That they would do a day's work for a penny. 'Take it. You have earned it. Take it and go your way. It is the legal amount.' It is then that the storyteller adds some words which have sounded harsh to his followers ever since. 'So the last shall be first, and the first last. For many may be called, but few are chosen.' It is Matthew the ex-tax-gatherer who records the parable. Why does it still ring with a certain unfairness?

The key lies in its opening. 'The kingdom of heaven is like unto a man who is a householder and who goes out early in the morning to hire men to work in his vineyard.' Putting across his kingdom had always been a far from easy task for Christ. But it was the heart of his teaching. The only kingdom those that listened to him longed for was that of King David long ago. It was a huge step for them to move from David's to Christ's kingdom, the passport to which was new birth, new allegiance, new values. It was, too, a laborious transition and not easy. New rules had to be learnt. If Christ was the Light, then his followers must carry his light, if he was the Word, then we must speak his word. Some of us will labour for the kingdom all our lives, from dawn to dusk, others just for an hour or two. But our reward will the same. In the parable we have that snatch of conversation.

'Why are you standing idle?'

'Because no one has hired us.'

'Then go you also into the vineyard.'

Many who followed Christ did not hang around waiting to be employed. They went off to do what he did. They healed and taught and extended his kingdom. It is always a great blessing of the Christian life to see people we know doing this – and usually with no idea that they are doing anything special. As for wages, these never enter their heads.

The pre-Lent days are filled with the humanity of Jesus. They are full of tales about efficient and inefficient farmers, about men and women who are too young to leave this beautiful springtime earth, Jairus's daughter, the lad from Nain, the Lord's own dear friend Lazarus, and who are given more life to enjoy it. We have no record of him raising dead old people. They had had their day. These stories sometimes mention the 'multitude', or human beings in the mass, and which he sees with 'compassion'. When we look at the churning Middle Eastern crowds on television it strikes us that little has changed in this respect since Jesus walked in Palestine. Humanity pours through Scripture, in mobs, in armies, in friendly groups, alone. It is a fragile passing show, dependent on God. That sea of faces which confronts us in the football stadium, and that single face which catches our eye in the street, reflect the face of God. The third Sunday before Lent could be called the Feast of the Creator. It points in all directions to the universe and to our habitat. It reverences the earth. It underlines the fact that 'It is he that hath made us, and not we ourselves.'

In Solitude He Sought Him

Here we all are, very quiet in the Lenten cathedral. No music, no movement, no light left of the early spring day. Just your stillness and my voice. We are just past Mothering Sunday, the Gospel for which is the feeding of the five thousand. There they all were, an enormous Middle Eastern crowd far from home and a meal, lured on by an irresistible talker, forgetting time, ignoring the miles, and now very hungry. Hunger breaks the spell which the great teacher had cast, but what to do? Andrew says hopelessly, 'There is a boy here who has five barley loaves, but what are they among so many?' Five barley loaves and two fishes, to be exact. I have often wondered how Andrew knew this. Also, why the boy did not run off and hide behind a rock and eat his packed lunch before some of these grown-ups fell on it like wolves? I have wondered how it felt to have it taken out of his hands and passed to the Lord. Who would have made the barley loaves? Mother, of course. Who had caught the fish? The boy? Andrew? The boy was a child of promise. Well, all children are that, but he was on the road to immortality sooner than most of us. His little meal satisfied everyone, including the great teacher perhaps, who knew all too well what hunger was and who had once cursed a fig tree because it had no fruit, The feeding of the five thousand ends on a miraculous note, as miracles do. But there is a final sentence or two which is apt to be left out when the story is retold. It is that there were certain men present who were so convinced of the Lord's divine power that they would have there and then crowned him king. But – and here comes our Lenten theme – 'he departed into a mountain alone.'

It is one of numerous occasions when Jesus gave those who wanted to make him an earthly ruler, the slip. 'He departed into a mountain alone.' The word 'solitude' does not appear in Scripture, but the word 'alone' does, many, many times. Because in Lent we tend to dwell on privation, on lonely suffering, I would like to direct our thoughts to the healing nature of solitude. Jung wrote, 'Solitude is for me a fount of healing which makes my life worth living. Talking is often a torment to me and I need many days of silence to recover from the futility of words.' Jung used solitude to recharge his batteries, to renew his spiritual strength. We need to do this, to be alone but not lonely.

During the Spanish civil war Roy Campbell and his wife managed to save the papers of St John of the Cross from being destroyed. They were the poems of a saint who was a master of solitude. St John was a tiny, humble man who did not think of himself as a poet at all. Now and then he would jot down some directions for those who were on the road to God, or make a note of what he had himself seen on the way, as he believed, to union with Christ. His Christ was the bridegroom of the Gospels – which made the poet the bride. When a woman told him that her prayer consisted of 'Considering the beauty of God and in rejoicing that he has such beauty', St John of the Cross found the imagery he needed for his poetry. It was that of the seeking lover – the seeking lover on both sides. The scenes in which the Lord and his saint search for one another are from the wild landscape of Toledo. These solitudes are filled with their love and desire for each other. Cathedrals are often huge solitudes for the seeker, especially at night when the footfalls of the sightseers die away. It is then that the arches and ceilings have something non-architectural to confide. St John of the Cross was not popular. He worked too hard, he was, they said, a crony of the overwhelming St Teresa of Avila. And he was, as some poets are, very accusative at times. He went to prison, but whether in his cell or by the river Guadalimer, his favourite outdoor spot, the blessed solitude was the same where he heard:

> The music without sound,
> The solitude which clamours,
> The supper that revives us and enamours.

As well as being Mothering Sunday the first Sunday in Lent is known as Refreshment Sunday because of the story of the miraculous picnic. There is pleasure in Lent. There are loaves as well as stones. There is the bell-clear speech of Christ as well as the undertones of the tempter. 'The wilderness and the solitary place shall be glad for them [the redeemed]; and their desert shall rejoice, and blossom like the rose' (Isa. 35.1).

The heart of the desert experience is that we should expect to discover something of our true selves there, both through unhappiness and a new-found happiness. However, part of the way through this time of self-examination, we are asked to take our eyes off the Lord's own pain in order to see that joy which it brought to the world. He was young and, as we say, 'with the whole of his life before him'. He was shown an alternative route to that which could only lead to the place of the skull. It was exciting and possible. Then the desert – the solitude – clarified everything, made plain the divine journey. Even if his natural terror of what he must come to shook his flesh, love drove out weakness. Every year we do our best to enter just a fraction into the sufferings of Jesus in the wilderness, to travel with him a few yards along the way to Calvary, this being our religious duty. We try – I try – now and then to get away from desert celebrities and mystics, away from saints and poets, just to taste solitude for myself – to see what it is like. To find out if it is all they say it is. A walk, a quiet room, the village church when nothing is going on, prayer minus words, silent songs, nursing the cat, getting lost in the cloud formations, or in Bach, listening to noiselessness, studying a spring flower or a bird in flight. Reading Isaiah. What a map-maker of the Christian's territory! Whilst frequently at worship in the Temple or in synagogue, Jesus taught the efficacy of solitary prayer, prayer without language in the lonely hills, prayer never overheard in locked rooms.

Writing is famously a solitary occupation. Whilst there are examples of poets and philosophers – mainly French – hard at work at café tables, most of us hide away and spend much of our existence in as soundless a room as we can find. The Orkney poet George Mackay Brown used to tell me how he spent his working day. Up early to write with a pen at his kitchen table, breakfast things pushed back to make a space, a blank wall facing him so as not to be beguiled by what lay outside the window. And then, after lunch, an hour or two in an armchair by a coal fire to 'interrogate silence', as he half-jokingly put it. Then a boisterous evening with fishermen and oilmen in the local. Working solitude, working silence and then working companionship. My own routine is not all that dissimilar, *sans* the pub. Although, unlike George's, my house is so isolated that the only passing traffic I might hear is a plane on its way to Stansted or Bernard on a tractor. Should I be interrogating silence it would most likely be from a flowerbed or during a long walk. Most of all as I walk.

For a Christian, solitude can be where he or she is least alone. The companionable Christ is often close at hand then. We daydream, we allow our thoughts to run free, we feel suddenly unpredictably happy, we have a realization of the value of often-neglected things which reintroduce themselves to us. Money takes a step backwards. Our bodies, even if they are not quite what they once were, feel good.

It is Lent but it is also springtime and it is ungrateful not to be elated as well as serious. 'Why are you so cast down?' asks the divine stranger who is catching up with us, the question he had asked those walkers along the Emmaus road who believed that God had left them in the lurch, not that they had left him in the greatest solitude there is, the grave. 'Where have you been these last days not to know this?' they asked him who had caught them up. 'It has been the talk of the town.' The walking Lord walked on, as he does to this day, the perfect filler of solitude, easy company, dropping into step and into conversation, and never quite the same person we meet at the altar. St John of the Cross found him as a bride finds the bridegroom, Mother Julian found him very sensible and kind, which was more than one could say of some of the Church's teachings then. George Herbert laid a place for him at the rectory dinner table. General Booth made thousands march beside him through the Victorian cities, trumpets blaring, banners blazing, yet each poor soul blessedly alone.

I have often wondered whether it was because of the hideous aloneness which the desert forced upon him that Jesus made it certain that his followers would never know such desolation. Or perhaps he was remembering David's sense of going under in Psalm 69: 'Save me, O my God, for the waters are come in even unto my soul. I sink in deep mire where there is no standing. Don't let it swallow me up ... In my thirst they gave me vinegar to drink ... I looked for some to take pity ... and for comforters ...

but I found none.' Never would a friend of Christ need to say this. Four times in St John's Gospel we are told, 'I will ask the Father to give you another Comforter and he will stay with you always . . . I will not leave you comfortless. I will come to you' (John 14.16–18).

We should recognize that the solitary place is a healing place. Nor need we be at all mystical about it. Go to the seashore in March. Go to the budding woods, as I did the other day. Sit in the park. Walk the footpaths. None of these places will be crowded in Lent. Each will be eloquent. Not long ago my Australian nephew took me to see the aborigines' dreaming places, special locations where one could be alone for a month or so. You watched the clouds or the waves or the birds and you *lived*. You might leave your mark on a rock or smooth out a hollow for your hip. We sat in such a dream place high up on a plateau above the Pacific Ocean and it seemed impregnated still with an ancient desert happiness, the happiness of those who knew something about seasons but nothing about clocks, and who valued stillness more than gold. 'In solitude he sought him. In solitude Christ guided his loved one through the shade.'

Mothering Sunday

A favourite walk for country people is often one which they don't have to make a journey to before beginning it. Thus my favourite walk in Wormingford is that which leads to Wissington. I just step from the farmhouse to the track and tramp my way via familiar field paths to the river, cross the pontoon bridge and there I am, in Wissington. My place-name dictionary tells me that it is one of those villages which were founded by women, like the delightfully named Sible Hedingham. Wissington, they say, was 'Wigsith's tun, or home'. Was it she who dedicated the church to Mary the mother of Jesus? Anyway, here is a motherly spot only two miles from my home, a near thousand-year-old church in, probably, a near thousand-year-old farmyard. A more harmonious group of sacred and workaday buildings it would be hard to find. Their footings, like plants which share a particular soil, seem to be struck in the local clay. Old friends, long enough dead not to give grief, speak to me from tombstones. If it is a warm day I take a rest on a bench commemorating a young organist who was killed in the Western Desert, a schoolmaster's son. If I have a sudden longing for the dream-inducing interior, I take a seat in the lovely, clumsy Norman nave to look once again at the ancient wall-paintings. They come and go in the damp plaster, apostles, angels, the Lord and his Mother, St Francis and his birds, a kind of old scrapbook made by children of faith.

A young artist, John Nash, and a young writer, Adrian Bell, once made a book entitled *Men and the Fields* about Wissington. It was 1938 and they were neighbours along the lane. I knew them when they were old. They too sat in the nave and Adrian wrote:

> Inside the church a great Norman arch is dominant, with its toothed design. One arch spans the whole, you look through it to the altar. The church is so small, the windows of the nave are no more than dream-holes, the wall so thick the light has the effect of being poured in through a funnel. The nave is secular in its barnlike simplicity: its silence but a pause in the labour of labouring men. But the arch transforms everything. Civilized, it supports easily a weight of time. Outside, much younger things look much older – the barns, cart-sheds, the farmhouse itself . . . they have that blunt dissolving look of an old haystack.

Curiously, maybe because of the church's dedication, plus in March a churchyard which is positively encased in celandine, Wissington at all times of the year emanates a kind of Annunciatory feeling whenever I arrive in it. I think of child workers in the market towns having a holiday for Mothering Sunday and hurrying home, picking primroses on the way, and with simnel cake being baked to welcome

Ewe anxiously calling her lamb

them. Simnel from simila, meaning fine flour. Kilvert-like scenes, and not all that long ago. And here for centuries the wandering gaze as the parson went on and on of boys and girls, and possibly mother herself, picking out Annunciation, Nativity, Flight . . . Pieta . . . fishing boats, that old Serpent over the north door. All the riverside folk were so at ease with their neighbours the Holy Family.

> A message came to a maiden young:
> The angel stood beside her,
> In shining robes and with golden tongue,

He told what would betide her;
The maid was lost in wonder,
Ah, how could she
Christ's Mother be . . . ?

All very nice, you will say, but we live now, not then. Not in some kind of holy archaeology or picturesque concept of rural life and rural faith. Christ's love for us is a continuum which cannot remain history. But he too possessed a family tree of fathers only – except for Ruth the gleaner who married farmer Boaz, the founders of his line. His advice to us is to neither look back all the time nor forward all the time, but to find time for the present. The present is what we *have*.

On Mothering Sunday we listen to two stories, one about an old man's recognition of a mother and child, the other about a woman who longs to be a mother. Hannah's husband doesn't quite understand. He tells her that he could not love her more than he does if she had given him many sons, so why worry about it? His other wife has proved his virility. He is satisfied. But Hannah is not. I have always thought that it is proof of her husband's huge respect for her that when at long last she does give birth to Samuel, he allows her to place him when still a baby in the charge of the far from reputable priests at the shrine up the hill. Hannah mothered her boy from afar, taking him a new coat each year. Like Mary centuries later, she accepted God's purpose for giving her a son, which was to lead his chosen people to a new stage of their national development. Samuel was to be the king-maker. God was to give him 'vision'. Poor old Eli at the shrine had been given two bad sons but not what a priest prayed for most – vision. I have often wondered what the mother of Eli's sons was like for them to have turned out such bad lots. Perhaps they loved her, and she them. Mothers continue to love their children even when they cause them pain. It is one of the best known facts of motherhood. Jesus caused his mother pain when he told her roughly, 'Do you not realize that I have to be about my Father's business?' He meant that 'business' for which he had come into the world. And Simeon, after recognizing the Christ-child in the Temple and telling Joseph and Mary that he thanked God for letting him live to see 'the glory of Israel', warned the young mother that her life would not be all joy. 'A sword shall pierce your soul.'

Our mothers were relieved and exultant when we were born. They had a song in their hearts, a song which continued during the stressful years of our growing up and of our necessary growing away from them in order to be ourselves and not dependent on them. Hannah, after giving birth to Samuel, sang a song which Mary remembered before she gave birth to Jesus. It may have been a traditional song for Jewish mothers. Hannah sang, 'The Lord maketh poor, and maketh rich, he bringeth low and lifteth up.' Mary sang, 'He hath put down the mighty from their seats, and exalted them of low degree.' She sang it to another mother-to-be, her cousin Elizabeth who was near to giving birth to John the Baptist. The meeting of these two ladies in the Judean hills is known as 'the Salutation' and it was a favourite subject for Italian artists. Much of the warmth of Christian motherhood comes to us via Italian art. Its 'Virgin and Child' pictures are able to show God in his mother's arms – and any baby being fed.

Jesus saw children as spiritually mature human beings. In order to enter his kingdom grown men and women had to recover this early spirituality, or at least some of it. In some ways we do not grow up, we grow away. Our mothers can see this happening but can do little about it. For in this sense they too grew away. But there is always the coming home. The prodigal son – came home. Long ago children came home on Mothering Sunday, walked to their native roots, sat maybe in the country church where they had been baptized, saw the familiar things, the big arch, the saints jostling in the painted windows, the bellringers at work, the candles in a draught. Heard the choir singing:

> The old man, meek and mild,
> The priest of Eli slept;
> His watch the Temple child,
> The little Levite kept.
> And what from Eli's sense was sealed,
> The Lord to Hannah's son revealed.

The Cup of Life

Passiontide, when we dwell on the mental suffering of Christ as the hour of his death approaches. The manner of this death was very terrible, and made deliberately so as a method of keeping disturbing men in order. No one alive in the Lord's day who benefited from this part of the Roman peace would have been ignorant of crucifixion. It was intended to be the most awful lesson possible for anyone who dared to upset such a peace. Crucifixion stared, not only the common criminal, but the public nuisance in the face. Jesus and his friends would have seen the crosses on the waste ground of cities. Those who hung on them would have been the poor and unimportant victims of a ferocious law. If you were 'somebody' and had been sentenced to death, you were executed with a sword. Or were told to take your own life in the privacy of your own house. No hanging between earth and sky as a lesson for all.

When Jesus, in his acute mental suffering, asked his Father to 'let this cup pass from me', it sounds to us that he may have heard about the ancient Greek method of execution when the condemned man had to drink poison – Socrates' death as willed by the state. 'If it be thy will, let this cup pass from me.' And then the marvellously brave,

'But thy will be done.' Only hours before Jesus had instituted the Cup of Life. He and his disciples, including Judas, had all drunk from it – the Cup of Life. But now, horror of horrors, the 'moment', as he called it, had arrived. Those who had drunk from his Cup of Life were outside there in the darkness, worn out, drained in another sense. He reproached them for falling asleep, for leaving him emotionally on his own at a time when he was so overwhelmed by what would happen to him that he sweated blood. Overcome too by the realization that humanity, then or in the future, would only be able to walk part of the way with him. And so he says, 'Sleep on.'

Right from the start the Church has done its level best to accompany Christ, to stay close to him, because of his immense loneliness in the garden. The main characters in the awful drama were taking up their positions, the pain-blunted soldiers, the Jewish high priest, the Roman judge, the alarmed mother, the frightened friends, the courageous Joseph from Arimathea. There were elements of hurry, of swift dispatch, of getting the wretched business over. The Passover was about to begin and corpses had to be out of sight. They defiled.

All this would have poured through the mind of the young teacher who was the Christ, the Redeemer of mankind. It was his 'passion', his mental agony. We do right to think about it. We all know something about ordeal, if only as spectators. We have seen the faces of those for whom there is no escape from the gas chamber, from the firing squad, or from a disease, maybe. It is in Jesus's realization that the cup cannot pass him without his drinking it to the dregs that we too become shaken by the inevitability of all that must happen to him. Accepting it meant not accepting that crude opiate, the sponge soaked in sour wine which executioners were allowed to press to the mouths of those they had tortured. Once the Lord had asked a woman for a cup of water from a foreign well and in the worldly-wise talk which followed he had assured her that he could give her a cup from which she could drink life itself. There would be no thirsting for what she had thirsted for ever again. She at first took him literally – what a blessing not to have to walk all this way to the well every day!

On Passion Sunday Christ walks to the source of this life – providing refreshment, his own voluntarily spilt blood. I often think of the two long walks to and from Calvary. One from the Judean hills, with the cross waiting, one to Emmaus, and between them that central destination too dreadful to think about. And yet it is this destination which we are asked to contemplate today, Passion Sunday, this suffering of Jesus as he brought himself to look towards Calvary.

For centuries we have sung the Passion of Christ, first as plainsong then as the profound musical statements made by Bach. And some of the Passion hymns are ages old and have become rich, dark, grand, sad vehicles for feelings which we would otherwise find it impossible to express. Isaac Watts took St Paul's words to the Galatians in order

to express them with simplicity in 'When I survey the won-
drous cross', and Isaiah's words in the great Passion choral
'O sacred head' leave us chilled and shocked. Also more
*com*passionate than we thought ourselves capable of being.
Here is not only God being defiled but a body like ours
being mutilated, and before our eyes. John Henry Newman,
a young priest preaching on the Passion in St Mary's,
Oxford, paused in his account of this suffering Christ and
added: 'And he to whom these things were done was
Almighty God.' A silence such as had never been known
before was said to have run through the crowded church.

We have got used to the crucifixion. It ceases to horrify
us. The body nailed to the tree hangs behind me as I speak
and I put it straight should I disturb it as I climb the pulpit.
As for the mind of Jesus as he approached such a death,
well none of us would presume to enter it. Gethsemane has
to be as deserted by us as by his disciples. Yet we do not
sleep and no longer do we have to be afraid of our association with him. Many in today's world would see us as
harmless followers of an old religion which has its beauties
and its irrelevance. Passiontide makes tough demands on
us, demands which go far beyond that undemanding faith-
fulness which an unfaithful time accuses us of possessing.
It tells us to look at hell instead of heaven. Hell as we create
it for one another.

The black and golden days ahead of us are crammed
with lessons. They hold, like a cup, the very essence of our
spiritual nourishment. They force us to face up to human

cruelty. As we know to our cost, it is not only the poor who are always with us, but the torturers. Where was the imagination of all those people who, even if he had been a common criminal, took the life of Jesus so horribly? But then, where was the imagination of all those people who ran the Nazi death camps? What we must not flinch from at Passiontide is the sight of a sentenced man being thrown to the pack. Wonderfully, at his last breath he exonerated all those who were engaged in his execution – 'They do not know what they are doing.' And this is the nub of the matter where cruelty to any living thing is concerned, those engaged in it either cannot feel, or cannot bring themselves to feel what the victim feels. One of Christ's least obeyed laws is that which said that whenever we injure or neglect another person, we injure or neglect him.

To contemplate should mean to gaze steadily and think deeply. When God created his world he looked at it and recognized that it was good. During Passiontide we try to gaze upon the sufferings of Jesus as he approached his death. The collect asks God to 'look upon his people'. And thus we have this double contemplation, of we ourselves looking as directly as we can at an agonized figure in the garden, not turning away, and of God looking hard yet lovingly at us. 'Go to dark Gethsemane', wrote James Montgomery, 'your Redeemer's conflict see. Watch with him one bitter hour.'

Ride On!

———◆———

If Good Friday is the most tragic day of the year and Easter the happiest, then Palm Sunday has to be the most poignant. It is also the most easily understood, for we are familiar with crowd adulation and national longings. The teaching which Jesus's earliest followers found hardest to understand was his repeated insistence that his kingdom was not of this world. The annual Passover feast in Jerusalem fed national longings. God had led his people out of bondage ages ago, would he not do so again? They crowded into their sacred capital, and not only Jews, but 'Greeks' – non-Jews – too. For a week it was *en fête*. The new Temple was all prepared for the great ceremonies. There was hubbub and joy. It was holiday. The Romans and their puppet king lay low. Unless there was riot or open challenge to their rule they appear to have tolerated the many curious religions of the empire. This one was strangely impressive and the Roman governor would be drawn to the extraordinary figure in the dock and would have discharged him but for threats to report him to Caesar for leniency. No governor must have a reputation for leniency – it was career death. And so he gave in to mob rule. It is brave in our day for a leader to stand up against tabloid rule.

But Pilate is nearly a week ahead. This is Palm Sunday. The streets echo with Zechariah's thrilling words, 'Behold, thy King cometh unto thee ... lowly, and riding upon an ass ... upon a colt the foal of an ass!' And so the amazing procession wound on its prophetic way, through the main gate, along the high ground, past the thronged inns and shops, the public buildings and up the Temple mount. And as it went its glorious way, the acclamation grew louder and louder. Both citizens and visitors were in an ecstasy of patriotic fervour and were intoxicated by a kind of longing to believe that the rider was their King. Although the Gospels do not mention it, we are right to decide that Jesus at this moment was a noble sight. Here was Christ the King with his royalty for all to see. It was the tradition that when a new king rode into his capital he should be mounted either on a horse or an ass. A horse meant that he would be a harsh ruler, an ass, a benign one. In a few days' time rough soldiers would amuse themselves at the expense of this pretender to a throne. He would be crowned all right – with a wreath of thorns. He would wear borrowed purple. They would pay him homage with spit. It would be a good joke to bow and scrape before him, to mock a man who had made a mockery of kingship. We can hear the loutish laughter to this day. We can also hear the weary voice saying, over and over again, 'My kingdom is not of the world.' It was not something which an occupied people wanted to hear.

And so on that pre-Passover day in springtime, with

Herod's newly built Jerusalem crammed with celebration – and longing – the crowds wished themselves to believe that David's descendant had arrived, had come to claim his crown. The wonderful teacher and healer was on his way to the throne of Israel. King Jesus. Branches were torn from the budding trees and strewn before him. His people spread their cloaks on the ground for the little colt to trot over with its delicate feet. King Jesus rode on and on and when at last he reached the Temple he behaved as if he should have been mounted on a horse. Bank counters had been set up in its courts for the lucrative business of selling birds and lambs for the altar. He overturned them, crying, 'This should be a house of prayer, not a den of thieves!' He wept, for the holiness of the Temple had long been contaminated with commercialism, and it broke his heart. Also there was something which told him that, rebuilt and lovely though it was, its days were numbered. The Romans would recognize it as a rallying symbol of revolt and would raze it to the ground.

It is a profoundly moving story. Christ's followers have never found difficulty in understanding it. What happened, and what must happen, is shockingly obvious. Pontius Pilate would have remembered the uproar and the dignity when, the following Friday, he ordered a label to be fastened to the cross. It was, 'Jesus of Nazareth the King of the Jews'. 'Say that he *called himself* "the King of the Jews"', they pleaded. 'Write my label in the main languages of the world!' commanded the Governor. To further protest he made his classic reply, 'What I have written, I have written.'

After the procession, and after cleansing the Temple, Christ retired to Bethany, a village just outside the city walls, to prepare himself for a longer and more terrible journey, and for the greatest triumph of all. The pomp, majesty and violence of the entry into Jerusalem haunts the Christian imagination. Knowing what was to come, we half wish that his reign of love could have begun at that moment and without the horror to come. But, as the old hymn says, 'Ride on, ride on in majesty! In lowly pomp ride on – to die!' The throne is a scaffold.

I used to hear the story of General Allenby's entry into Jerusalem. My father used to tell it to us as children. After Gallipoli his regiment, the 5th Suffolks, became part of the force led by General Allenby to destroy Turkish rule in Palestine. Allenby took over in June 1917 and after battles in which 28,000 soldiers lost their lives, he intended to make a victor's entry into Jerusalem on 11 December that same year. He rode ahead of his troops on a white horse with flags flying and bands playing. It was to be very grand. He had helped to destroy the ancient and enormous Ottoman Empire. There were plans afoot to bring the Jews back to Palestine. The military procession marched to the gates of Jerusalem, my nineteen-year-old father somewhere in it, when, quite suddenly, there was a ragged halt and confusion. Something unrehearsed. Because, as he reached the gates, General Allenby remembered something, how Christ had entered Jerusalem on a colt, not a horse, on his way to bring *his* kingdom into human hearts. Allenby came to a stop and dismounted, and walked into Jerusalem. The trumpets and drums were silenced, the flags lowered, as he entered the Holy City.

So far as the Church is concerned, Palm Sunday is the origin of its processions. If we had lived here during the Middle Ages we would have processed from country church to country church, singing 'Hosannah in the highest!' and Bishop Fortunatus's 'The royal banners forward go!', cutting pussy willow wands – no dried palms from Palestine in those days – and meeting on our way Palm Sunday processions in every lane. We would have remembered, then as now, that it was a man as well as God who was riding to the kingdom.

Shepherd Sunday

O n Easter Two, the Gospel is – or was – 'Jesus said, I
am the good shepherd: the good shepherd giveth his
life for the sheep.' The animal most mentioned in our faith
is the sheep or the lamb. And not surprisingly when the
Old Testament is the history of a shepherd nation, a tribe
of herdsmen always at first moving on to fresh pasture.
Although it had concluded that there could only be one
God it dared not say his name. It approached him through
blood, lamb's blood. We draw back from such an altar, as
did Jesus. For him sheep and shepherd and ritual sacrifice
were more than old rites and symbols. He is unequivocal,
indeed overwhelming when he speaks on this reverse
order of things. 'I am the good shepherd, and know my
sheep, and am known of mine . . . and I lay down my life
for the sheep. And other sheep I have, which are not of
this fold; them also I must bring, and they shall hear my
voice, and there shall be one fold, and one shepherd'
(John 10.14–16 KJV).

These are beautiful, understandable and reassuring
words, and they comfort us. They also alert us, startle us
to the fact that if Christ is the good shepherd, then it must
follow that there are bad shepherds. And of course he

mentions them. He calls them 'hirelings', meaning people who are never committed to their task. Should there be trouble, 'the hireling runs away because he *is* a hireling, and doesn't care for the sheep'. The hireling lacks love and responsibility and is disconnected.

The image of Jesus as our knowing, caring shepherd is the one we love most. It is April and although the weather is wet and cold, and miserable for lambing, the new-born lambs run and leap happily in the new grass. I have been watching Paul's lambs, how one minute they are dancing under the bare oaks, the next hurtling themselves into their mothers' warmth. Their new cries are often like the cries of children. How at our mercy they are, these Christ symbolizing creatures. How they touch our hearts, these ewes and their offspring. We are unable to escape the questions they pose. Living animal, living symbol, living Word.

It was Jesus's cousin John who challenged the old pastoral religion by crying out, 'Behold the Lamb of God!' as he approached. He was telling this transcendent fact to none other than the man who would become John the apostle. These two Johns would, between them, establish their Lord as the ultimate sacrificial Lamb. Never again would humanity need to cringe towards God via bloody altars. Because, as the Easter Day preface assures us, 'He is the very Paschal Lamb, which was offered for us, and has taken away the sin of the world. Who by his death has destroyed death.'

'O Lamb of God,' we plead, 'who takes away the sins of the world, have mercy upon *us*.'

MN

Black lamb

The Paschal lamb provided a feast. It was sacrificed in the Temple on the afternoon of 14 Nisan, or mid-April, ritually offered to God, then taken by the family which had presented it back home and eaten for supper that same night. All this in memory of the saving of a pastoral nation from slavery. St Paul refers to this when, writing to the church which he has founded at Corinth, he says, 'Christ *our* passover is sacrificed for us, therefore let us keep the feast. Not with the old leaven, nor with the leaven of malice and wickedness, but with the unleavened bread of sincerity and truth' (1 Cor. 5.7).

What does the Lamb himself say to us this second Sunday after Easter? He says that although he went like a lamb to the slaughter, that he lives! 'I am the resurrected one and your Shepherd!' He was no temporary carer, no hireling. 'I am the good shepherd who gave his life for you. I never ran away when the terrible sacrificial moment came – I never will. I am constancy. And I know you all – because you are mine. Once you left me and got hurt and frightened. You got lost. But now you are returned, in Peter's words, "To the Shepherd and Bishop of your souls".' The word 'bishop' comes from the Greek word for 'overseer'. And bishops, of course, carry shepherds' crooks to show their rescuing authority.

We hear of no sheepdogs in the Bible. Neither do its shepherds drive their flocks before them, but lead them. 'Lead us, heavenly Father, lead us . . .' Just imagine those prince-shepherds of old Israel, each with his crook for emergencies, striding ahead of his vast flocks, his wives and children and servants following. When at last these nomads settled in one place and made towns and villages, the shepherds themselves still had to wander in the hills to those feeding grounds such as we see on the Welsh and Scottish mountains. And it was there that they 'watched'. The danger was not so much stealers as wild animals. But having made a pen and lit a fire, there was often little more to do – except watch, of course. And then another kind of watchfulness would take over, the kind which we call 'contemplation'. The shepherds, like the shepherd-king

David, became poets and mystics. They wrote the psalms. They named the stars. They recognized important truths. Jesus was able to trace his family back to the shepherd-king David.

> The Lord is my shepherd, therefore can I lack nothing.
> He shall feed me in a green pasture, and lead me forth
> beside the waters of comfort.

There are those, of course, who despise religion as a comfort – as a prop, as they call it. But Christ will have none of this. He leaned on his friends, depended on them, and they in turn supported him in his humanity. Life is not easy. On the contrary, it is often hard, complicated and difficult. Each of us at some time puts a foot wrong and needs rescuing. But although the Good Shepherd leads us, we also have to follow as best we can. Isaiah, the great moral leader of a shepherd people, urged them to 'Seek the Lord while he may be found, call upon him while he is near.' For there were times when the shepherd strode far ahead and the flock dawdled, grazing this way and that, losing all direction. But does he press on regardless? Does he say, 'Well, I have got most of the flock following on. What does it matter if a lamb or two can't make it?' In Jesus's parable the shepherd first takes care that the flock is safe, then he turns back for the lamb which is missing. He lifts it on his shoulders and, later, when his friends ask him what he is so cheerful about, he tells them, 'Share my happiness. I managed to find and bring home that sheep which had gone – that sheep which went astray.'

Finding what was lost is always a matter of celebration in the Bible. A woman loses one of her ten silver ornaments and turns the house upside down before she finds it. She has to celebrate the recovery with her neighbours. It is probable that the coin was part of her dowry.

A long time ago a friend of mine lost his daughter to the Moonies. He had five other children but he moved heaven and earth, as they say, to bring her safely home. And when, after the greatest difficulties, he did find her, she had to be helped to find *him*, for the sect had wiped him from her memory.

A year or two ago my neighbour Mr Brown was walking over a field when he found a perfect Bronze Age axe-head lying on the newly ploughed earth. It had worked itself up. Someone had lost it in *c.* 700 BC. It was as new and unmarked as when it left the forge. But what a loss! I imagined the owner going back on his tracks, his eyes glued to the ground, and never of course imagining for one moment that it would take another farmer to find it when three thousand years had passed.

Now and then we lose faith in someone and have to set out to find that faith once more. Sometimes we lose faith itself and are devastated, or puzzled. But Christ is a searcher and a finder. The father of the prodigal son was also the father of a faithful stay-at-home son and he could have said of the wastrel, 'Good riddance to bad rubbish!' Or he might

just have given the prodigal up and taken no further responsibility for him. But what did he do? He *watched out*
for him. He searched the road every day for a sign of him.
And then it happened. The far-distant speck, the dirty tramp
of a young man coming nearer and nearer, ashamed, frightened, and with his set speech of apology. And did the father
wait for the embarrassing meeting? He *ran* to meet his lost
son and kissed him, brushing aside the grovelling words
and calling for clean clothes and a homecoming party.

Faith teaches us in all sorts of ways how to deal with
loss, and in whatever form it comes. It tells us to unite
recovery with celebration.

A Saxon Tragedy

 — decorative divider

There is a remarkable novel by Willa Cather called *Death Comes for the Archbishop*. The history of the Church shows death coming to an archbishop quite frequently when his faith got in the way of politics or his king's needs. Thomas Becket is the most famous victim of this clash between Church and state. But I have always been fascinated by a predecessor of his, named Alphege, who met an horrific end when he refused to ransom himself at the expense of his poor tenants. His captors clubbed him to death after a drunken spree, killing him with beef bones. He was fifty-eight. Although this was a good age in the year AD 1012, there was something about Archbishop Alphege which tells us that he had not finished his task – that he was still a man of promise with much more to do. Like Archbishop Luwum of Uganda, Alphege had the misfortune to be working for God during one of those periods when a nation slips back into barbarity. We ourselves have witnessed such things many times. Alphege met his grotesque end on a chilly April day on a boat on the Thames. When I see his name on the calendar I find him stepping from the list of martyrs in a very lively fashion. He appears in the round and not in some flat picture from an ancient holy book.

He seems to be telling me, 'Let the world know more about me than the manner of my murder.'

One of the hazards of being a saint was to be dragged from a cell and made to sit on a bishop's chair, no matter if your head was good for prayer and no good at all for Church business. Some of the Celtic priests in particular dreaded any reputation they might have as a spiritual person becoming widely known, for it might mean having to exchange their beloved seashore, with its birds and solitude, for a throne. But because society's ideal is to be governed by those who possess the highest spiritual qualifications, this is what sometimes occurred. As we know, it did not work out on one famous occasion.

Henry II made his boyhood friend Tom Becket Archbishop of Canterbury believing that, as the trusted companion of his wild exploits, he would see that the Church did not get in the way of politics. What a mistake. Made head of the Church, Becket switched masters. In Peter's first letter we have the apostle saying, 'Honour all men, love the brotherhood, fear God, honour the king.' Honouring kings comes last on the list of what a Christian sometimes has to do. Jesus himself had reminded his friends that no one can have two masters.

Archbishop Alphege knew only one master, Christ himself; knew only one law, that given by Christ; accepted only one authority, that of his Lord. 'I should think so too!', we might say, 'him being the Archbishop of Canterbury.' But, as with many other great men, his position laid him open to a special violence. He certainly showed a special courage when his enemies caught him, knowing full well the terrible things they could do to him. Again we remember modern martyrs such as Dietrich Bonhoeffer, hanged by the Gestapo at Flossenbürg in 1945. Alphege was a Saxon nobleman who had given up everything to live simply in the countryside and pray to God. He built himself a little hut in the ruins of Bath and there he would have stayed had he had his way. But England was in turmoil due to the Danish raiders and their blackmail termed 'Danegeld', and the Church had become a particular target. It required strong leadership. Alphege knew nothing about leadership in the ordinary sense but his spiritual strength was obvious. So they forced him from his cell and made him Bishop of Winchester. He was thirty, the same age as Jesus when he left home to preach God's kingdom. Twenty years later Alphege was Archbishop of Canterbury.

The Danish raiders then demanded the then enormous sum of £48,000 to stop their burnings and massacres. It was pay up or else! Alphege held a council at which he reminded everyone of the laws of a Christian civilization, and how that they must prevail at all cost in the face of lawlessness. The king was so frightened of the Danes that he agreed to pay the ransom, and the Danes seized his Archbishop as a hostage to make sure that he did. They held poor Alphege on a ship anchored off Greenwich for seven months, and eventually murdered him during a drunken feast. He was actually put out of his agony by a young man he had secretly confirmed the day before.

Was it all in vain, this brave gesture not to make a deal with evil men? This setting up of a council of decency and wisdom? This becoming poor after being rich for the Lord's sake? This entire life which Alphege had chosen? Far from it. It was said that this Archbishop's death brought the country to its senses. Not long after King Cnute acknowledged that Alphege had been the man who had the nerve, as well as the spiritual authority, to halt what the psalmist described as 'the madness of the people'. In Alphege we recognize someone who constantly, sadly – and triumphantly – reappears in history. King Cnute owed much to Alphege and he acknowledged it in the customary way by giving him a magnificent burial. He had honoured God, so the king honoured him.

History for us is a perplexing matter. We use it now as an ever-fascinating source of entertainment. I do myself. We create theme parks where we can visit our local history. Old houses enthral us. Archaeology has us riveted. We immerse ourselves in historical films and novels, we throng our museums. Now and then I have to travel on the Circle Line and the train is packed, mostly with young people who dash off it at Tower Hill station as they head, full of excitement, for what was once the most dreaded prison of all and its blood-drenched drama. At the same time we can trivialize the past. We can view it falsely and turn away from its realities because of their being so shocking – or absurd. 'How can people have been so wicked or cruel – or ridiculous?' we ask ourselves. Thank goodness we are living in the twenty-first century! And then we pause. How different was Archbishop

Alphege's fate to that of our martyrs? Our hostages? Our Bonhoeffers and Luwums? To remind us we have that row of contemporary victims of 'the madness of the people' recently set up over the west door of Westminster Abbey, on the whole, men and women who did not see themselves as important. Their Lord was mocked and injured by clowning soldiers, his friend Alphege by drunken warriors, but the sanity of Christ and those who died for it remains.

Here is the prayer which Dietrich Bonhoeffer wrote on the eve of his execution in a Nazi prison.

O God, early in the morning I cry to you.
Help me to pray
And to concentrate my thoughts on you;
I cannot do this alone.

In me there is darkness,
But with you there is light;
I am lonely, but you do not leave me;
I am feeble in heart, but with you there is help;
I am restless, but with you there is peace.
In me there is bitterness, but with you there is patience;
I do not understand your ways,
But you know the way for me . . .

Restore me to liberty,
and enable me so to live now
that I may answer before you and before men.
Lord, whatever this day may bring,
Your name is praised.

Brother Nature

In 1225, the year before he died, St Francis sat in the garden of his little chapel near Assisi and wrote a hymn in praise of God as he is revealed in nature. He called it, 'Brother Sun and all his Creatures'. In it he relates himself to the natural world. He is brother to the sun, brother to the wind, brother to the trees and flowers, brother to the birds and animals, brother to all creation. Like his Lord, Francis had moved away from the concept of the natural world being a kind of larder for the benefit of mankind to that of a shared existence. Inherent in Christ's experience of the countryside is his wonder and delight in everything he sees, the crops, the blooms, the scenery, the creatures. His is a natural response to nature. He picks and chews corn as he walks, he is sorry for the small birds which are being caught for sacrifice, he points out rather gleefully that, do what he may, no king can match the glory of wild flowers.

The spring has come. It floods the church. A divine hand is familiarly at work in what we now call our local ecology, that careful relationship between organism and environment. Recent disasters and mishaps have reminded us what occurs when we take too drastic or greedy a hand in agriculture and upset this relationship. There is a new reverence for nature but it is no longer religious, or not entirely so as it was in Francis's day. The lens has revealed things above and below which his and later generations could never have imagined. But still the *Benedicite* manages to cover them, if not show them as we are now accustomed to see them. Science and holy song manage to fit together.

This being a praise address, I do not intend to repeat what we now know only too well, which is that we must all be preservationists now. What I want to emphasize is the continuing sacredness of the countryside. What is St Francis saying in his natural catalogue of love? It is 'relate, relate!' That great creation poem called Genesis which we read early in the year speaks of something quite different. It speaks of us as lords of creation. In Genesis human beings rule nature. Sitting in his Italian garden and near to leaving it, St Francis, aged forty-four, sees only family connections, including sister death.

Just below my old farmhouse, visible in February through the bare trees, is Wiston church with its flashing weathervane. I often walk to it across the river and sit inside it to stare at the Norman wall-paintings. My favourite is on the north wall above where the pulpit used to be. St Francis is preaching to the birds who are all turned to the east and paying attention. They say that this picture was painted only twenty years or so after his death, which proves how swiftly legends fly about the world. Generations of village folk, as they listened to their priests, would have recognized, not a fanciful saint talking to blackbirds, but a lesson on

Three jays

affinity. They might well have walked home saying 'Good day' to brother lark, brother oak, and sister moon, should it be after Compline. They might well have told themselves, 'We are all in it together.' In what? In life on earth.

Writers sometimes break out into the joy of being alive. Few could beat a young Herefordshire clergyman, Thomas Traherne. When he was a boy he thought:

> The corn was orient and immortal wheat, which never should be reaped, nor was ever sown. I thought it had stood from everlasting to everlasting. The dust and stones of the street [in Hereford] were as precious as gold. The gates were at first the end of the world, the green trees when I saw them first through one of the gates transported and ravished me, their sweetness and unusual beauty made my heart to leap, ... they were such strange and wonderful things. The men! O what venerable and reverend creatures did the aged seem! Immortal cherubims! And young men glittering and sparkling angels, and maids strange seraphic pieces of life and beauty! Boys and girls tumbling in the street, and playing, were moving jewels. I knew not that they were born or should die. But all things abided eternally as they were in their proper places. Eternity was manifest in the light of the day, and something infinite behind everything appeared ... The city seemed to stand in Eden, or to be built in Heaven. The streets were mine, the temple [he means Hereford Cathedral] was mine, the people were mine ... the skies were mine, and so were the sun and

moon and stars, and all the world was mine, and I
the only spectator and enjoyer of it!

This is a famous passage. It takes us back to our own
childhoods when we burst out of the house on a summer's
day. Traherne lived during the seventeenth century when
life was brief. He would die aged thirty-six. He preached
enjoyment of God's creation. He found nature ravishingly
beautiful. He said that we must 'want like a god and be
satisfied like God'. We should *want* the world which God
made, look for it, see it in all its variety and splendour. We
should search it out this very moment – for there is no
time to lose. He wrote:

> When I came into the country, and being seated
> among silent trees, had all my time in my own hands,
> I resolved to spend it all, whatever it cost me, in search
> of happiness, and to satiate that burning thirst which
> nature had enkindled in me from my youth.

There were times in the history of the Church when an
appreciation of nature was condemned, and the blessings
provided naturally by plants were forbidden, and those who
understood them, persecuted. The Church was scared of
Pantheism, or the recognition of God in mountains, rivers,
woods, etc. Yet some of its greatest saints 'saw' God in
nature, saw him more clearly there than anywhere else. Had
not Christ himself told his followers that he would be present in their natural food of bread and wine? Did he not
walk on real earth, put up with real bad weather while

sailing, did he not watch foxes, sheep, fish and sparrows? The earthy-ness of the Lord's teachings is often so pungent that we can almost smell rural Palestine. *We* nowadays talk of what we call 'the real world'. Jesus was entirely within the real world of his day, and he loved and valued it. When he had to explain his 'kingdom' to his friends he did not use unearthly analogies. He said it was like mustard seed, wheat, a garden, a vineyard.

We do not have to be taught to love our native scene. It is as natural a part of our affection as our families. Whilst there were periods when it was dismissed in favour of the life to come, and called 'a vale of tears', we now know that it is nothing of the kind. It is, as Traherne said, a world 'to be delighted in and highly esteemed'. I have often thought that some of the big questions which God will put to us might be, 'Why did you not enjoy it more, my beautiful world, my wonderful creation? Why did you not praise where I had put you – that spot which you called your "environment"? Why did you so often spoil it? Why did you sometimes think that you were "above" it? Why did you spend so much of your short life in "getting and spending" as Wordsworth said? And so little time in just looking?'

Jesus and his companions were lucky to have that marvellous handbook of nature-praise, the Psalms, in which gratitude for the world about them spills over into an appreciation of everything they saw. Including of course the night sky. For it was those 'watching' shepherd-poets who named the stars. Our good earth is the gift of God.

His incarnation brought him into his own gift, to feel it, to smell it, to touch it. The old writers called nature 'God's handywork', a homely name for it.

Rogation – The Asking Time at Little Horkesley

During our many Rogations here we have often, and understandably, behaved as if we were doing our best to breathe new life into an old custom. As with the harvest festival, it hasn't been easy to reconcile our combined fields with those in the harvest hymns, or one individual's work with that of the whole village, reaping and binding from dawn to dusk. These rural church ceremonies do still have their relevance, and certainly their sentiment, but they do also require quite a lot of imagination if we are to apply them to the present.

Well, this year it is different. The countryside is slowly emerging from a disaster. Country people – and animals – have been ruined or injured or destroyed in a way which none of us is likely to forget. In time to come 2001 will be known as a plague year, a year of what the old prayer calls 'dearth'. A year when it rained and rained, and where here, the normally driest corner of these islands, the fields puddled to such an extent that hundreds of acres remained unseeded. A year when disease ran its horrible course. A year when it was unbearable to watch its progress on television, a year when we all had to rethink our attitude towards farm animals and to agriculture generally. It all made us feel vulnerable and helpless. For a few months we have known what it was like to be our farming ancestors as tempest and sickness hit them.

And now, thank God, this distress to us and to the animal world has at long last run its course. It is late April and, although not very warm, the sun is out and everything we see is a kind of English perfection. Even our ambitious pond has remembered its limits. As for the spring flowers and the nesting birds, they are plentiful and wonderful. But we have had a sharp check to our sense of being in sole charge. We have been faced with the chilling realization of not knowing what to do. We did our scientific and financial best but something stronger and beyond us ran before us, just as such rural disasters did in the time of Thomas Hardy. It rained and rained. The sheep and the cattle burned every night on our television screens and the land was wounded. This bad business has shaken us.

This is the asking time and we might begin by asking forgiveness for any hubris we may have shown in our control of nature. For we have seen that there must be times when we are no longer in control – when matters are taken out of our hands. When the weather assumes control and there is nothing that we can do about it.

Today's Gospel begins,

> Verily, verily I say unto you, whatsoever ye shall ask the Father in my name, he will give it to you. Ask, and ye shall receive, that your joy may be full. These

things have I spoken to you in proverbs ... that in
me ye might have peace ... Be of good cheer.

(John 16.23–33 KJV)

This morning we ask for the normality of field and pasture,
for being able to return to a healthy, workable scene.

Rogation takes place where we belong. Christ was driven
out from where he belonged and was often shocked to find
himself homeless. His people took care to establish their
local boundaries. The boundary between Little Horkesley
and Wormingford runs alongside my garden hedge. It is in
the form of a medieval ditch, very deep and still churning
with flood water. The Rogation processions from both villages would have once marked it, perhaps meeting each
other on the way. They would have listed a tree here, a
stone there, a bend in the river, some oddity or feature in
the landscape. The New Testament nearly always tells us
where its characters come from. Peter and James from Galilee, Paul from Tarsus, Mary from the fishing village of
Magdala, Cleopas from Emmaus, Jesus from Nazareth. During Rogation we walk in a parish into which few of us
actually belong, except by right of the electoral roll. Yet the
walk has a way of returning us to our native place because
it symbolizes a common geography of nourishment for body
and spirit.

These past twenty or so years have educated us in what
we should see, and taught us to call it our environment.
They have extended our vision and thus our 'belonging'.
The camera shows us the ocean floor, the genetic process

of a seed, an eagle hatching its eggs, the mating of lions, the movement of the stars, a flower – flowering – an insect's eyes. As we look at these things we recognize that they are the fractional marvels of an amazing natural system which has become threatened by human so-called progress. The recent misfortunes have shown us how delicately balanced nature is, how easily damaged, how needful of our care. We have not quite reached the stage of devouring all the fruit of knowledge in the garden but in just a few generations humanity senses that it has advanced to within a step or two behind God.

Some of the early missionaries to these islands got themselves into a theological confusion about what they found here. River gods, forest gods, spirits of place, sacred groves. Pope Gregory told his emissary St Augustine, 'Do not cut down the sacred trees, reconsecrate the holy wells to Christ.' Churches were built on sites which had been revered for ages. People saw a continuity of sacredness, saw Christ instead of Woden. But as we know it was a policy which would run into future difficulties. The time would come when people would practice a double religion. Christ would be the heavenly faith, nature the earthly faith. Christ would heal miraculously, nature scientifically. The Church denounced the healing which nature provided, the medicine of plants, and the like. It was a policy which led to much persecution and blindness towards the environment.

St Francis was one of those who corrected the Christian attitude to nature. 'Enjoy every minute of your life here', he told his followers. 'The creatures are your brothers. The snow is your sister. Everything is related to us. We are all part of the divine family!' He wrote a poem exhorting creation to bless its Creator.

> *O ye works of the Lord, bless ye the Lord*
> O ye Sun, Moon, Showers, Dew, Winter, Summer,
> Frost, Cold, Ice, Snow, Nights, Days,
> Light, Darkness, Mountains, Green things,
> Wells, Seas, Whales, Birds, Beasts – bless ye the Lord!

Then he adds,

> *O ye humble men of heart, bless ye the Lord,*
> *Praise him and magnify him for ever.*

You holy and humble men of heart ... We are holy, or whole, when we look around our village, respect what we see, and tell ourselves. 'This landscape is part of me. So is this bird in the cherry tree and that mole in the lawn. So is that cat, that running horse, this waterlogged cornfield, those skies which John Constable saw, this air.' When they were marooned abroad for years at a time, exiles longed for nothing so much as a breath of their native air.

Jesus was so appreciative of his native countryside. His teaching is filled with references to it. He notices its plants, its animals and birds, its all kinds of weather, its calm places and its wild places. From hospitable Bethany to the wilderness. We are about to set off to see the things which have made it possible for people to live on this rise above the Stour for many centuries, the water, the crops, the cattle, the orchards, the gardens, and finally this church itself, bombed to smithereens in 1940, risen from the rubble in 1958. And as we walk and pause at each symbolic site, we shall sing praises and then *ask*. 'Ask and it shall be given you', said Christ. Flood and disease have given our rural self-sufficiency a hard knock. The countryside is not as it was when we walked this way a year ago. Who would have thought that it would be a treat to see a few sheep on a meadow? Here is an old prayer from the time when nobody in a village took anything for granted.

> Father, from whom all good things do come, grant to us, thy humble servants, that by thy holy inspiration, we may think those things that be good, and by thy merciful guiding may perform the same.

The Scottish Funeral

—————◆—————

A phenomenon of twentieth-century East Anglian farming is that some of its best land fell into disuse and wretchedness until it was brought back to life – by young Scots. I called these adventurers 'the Northern invaders' in *Akenfield*. Down they swept from their Lowland farmtouns, with their poor soil and poverty, to the rich clays of Norfolk, Suffolk, Essex and Cambridgeshire. Not only did these Scots bring back to life our farms, of which they became tenants before owning them, but they breathed new life and vitality into our villages. The Scots are the most powerful emigrants which these islands have produced, and they are certainly the most heartsick-for-home travellers, never entirely integrated where they choose to settle, and so they stay, like our old neighbour and friend, distinctive.

William Brown was born on an Ayreshire farm on Michaelmas Day just a hundred years ago. And he could say – indeed, he did say, for he was wonderfully articulate about what had happened to him all his long life – that he had witnessed the whole history of modern agriculture, from the kind of dairying which we read about in a Thomas Hardy novel to that of today's Common Agricultural Policy. All of it had passed before his eyes and through his hands.

I remember once needing to know how they reared the sheep on Romney Marsh before the last war, and it was 'Ask Mr Brown'. He would ask me to look up the meaning of certain Gaelic words in the glossary to my Robert Burns poems, because when you leave home aged three some of its meaning gets left behind. But very little of what he had seen and heard in a century of fields and meadows had slipped out of his memory, and so he was good to listen to. For many years he and Mr Gray, another ancient Scotsman, sat together at the back of this church in what they liked to call 'Farmers' Pew', and I often found myself thinking of the struggles and triumphs, like 'a tale that is told' that had brought them to Wormingford and Little Horkesley.

In 1901, when William Brown was a little boy, his father and two Ayrshire dairymen neighbours hired a special train for ten pounds, filled it up with everything which they possessed, their ploughs, their stock, their chattels, their families, and came to eastern England. The Browns eventually settled on a farm at Beacon Hill near Ongar. It was four times the size of the one which they left behind in Scotland. And there they worked with new hopes. It would be seventy years before William saw Ayrshire again but his parents, his mother especially, kept in touch with their roots. She was a Highlander and was never reconciled to our modest scenery.

Here there had been an abandonment of the farms. It was called 'the flight from the land'. The depression which had set in during the 1870s had created a bankrupt situation.

Before the First World War farms were almost given away or fell into ruin. It was not only the Lowland Scots, but their wives and daughters who pulled them round. William told me that, for all this, we East Anglians would mock them for their efforts and dub them 'cowkeepers'. Of course, what these hardworking incomers challenged was rural inertia. But it was a tough time and William saw bankruptcy, distress, suicide. He would also see the second agricultural revolution which, beginning with the 'War Ag.' as it was called, brought about the prosperity and mechanized farming which we have today, a farming almost without farmworkers. We – he and I – would talk about this roller-coaster of an industry, all ups and downs.

There was a certain wholeness of William's experience of country life which made him a natural philosopher. Sitting with me about once a week in my old farmhouse, I used to marvel at his memory and the extent of his knowledge. He drove his car well into his nineties, his dog leaning out of the window. And he took to sitting in it when he came to a beautiful view, particularly in the Stour Valley.

His father remained at Beacon Hill until 1905 then moved to a five hundred acre farm called Wyfields. It was from there that Williams walked to Orsett school. It was a magnificently wooded Essex, deeply rural still. In it the 'Northern invaders' formed their own community. They became in fact a kind of East Anglian–Scots clan – as can be proved by their descendants now filling this church. So great was the attraction of our farms to the Lowlanders that young farmtoun men – some of your grandfathers, no doubt – would walk from Ayrshire to Suffolk. William told me that one of the reasons why they remained clannish was because the locals rather looked down on them. I have always believed that they found the determination of these arrivals rather upsetting.

When William returned to Ayrshire after seventy years he took his grandsons with him. They went to look at a memorial to a Covenanter ancestor who had been executed by Claverhouse which had been set up on a lonely moor. William was amazed when I sang him the old song, 'To the Lords of Convention 'twas Claverhouse who spoke'. We had been taught it at school but I can't remember why. Fragments of poems, scraps of tunes, hang around in all our heads, making small connections but little sense. Something of his stern Presbyterian faith certainly hung around in William's head.

In 1917 with agriculture subsidized because of the war, the Browns moved to Maldon Hall, where William drove his first tractor, a Fordson. When the war was over he got a job as factor to Sir George Watson, who founded the Maypole Dairies. Sir George had himself begun life as a Northamptonshire farm boy. He and William got on well together and stayed with each other for twenty years. In 1949 he came into our orbit here at Little Horkesley, already over fifty, but with nearly fifty more years to come. In fact he arrived at Michaelmas, the classic date for a farm move, and on his birthday. He loved the hilly acres of Malting

Farm and the glimpse of the river below. He was amused when his next-door neighbour, the artist John Nash, called this landscape 'the Suffolk–Essex Highlands'.

Our memory of William is of 'Grandpa', whether we were related to him or not. He spent his last days with Colin and Zoë in his big East Anglian 'long-house', Dairy Farm, Colin so skilfully rebinding ancient books, although, said Grandpa, he never started work until halfway through the morning. 'But just think,' I said, 'how long Colin works when he does get up.' William died in his own bed with his children and grandchildren around him, just as a farmer-patriarch should. He took with him a whole history of farming such as one would now only find in a book. I was too old to call him 'Grandpa', so goodnight, Mr Brown.

The Massachusetts Connection

'Thinking means connecting things', said G. K. Chesterton, and an important part of a writer's function is to do just that, to make a connection between past and present, between the generations, between faiths and cultures, between politics and fates. The connections we have to make on this particular Rogation day are far-flung. Usually they are no further than our village boundary which we perambulate asking God for a good harvest – or thanking him for a good bus service. But today, with the ancient church filled with American guests, we connect ourselves with what happened here over fifty years ago when, on St Andrew's Day 1943, the USAAF began to operate from our airfield. Began to explore our countryside, began to meet our girls, began, some of them, to come to this church. What a tremendous role the level fields of East Anglia played during the last war. Waldingfield, Mildenhall, Bentwaters, Debach, Lakenheath, Wormingford, our places which have become places which are still a part of the lives of thousands of American citizens. Old now, they revisit them, driving slowly down the runways along which they once sped, opening the doors of pubs where they once sang, reading the names of friends they once knew.

These airfields were constructed on the very same fields and pastures farmed by men and women who left England in the 1630s for a new life in Massachusetts. In less than a dozen years no fewer than 16,000 emigrants from East Anglia had sailed away to New England, an enormous group considering the low population figures of that time. Their local leader was a lawyer named John Winthrop. He came from Groton, a few miles from here. He was forty-one, an intelligent, sensitive man who would found Boston and govern the Massachusetts Bay Colony for the rest of his life. He is such a familiar figure to Suffolk people like myself, that I continue to think of him as a neighbour just up the road. When I was in Boston, which he named after Boston in Lincolnshire, the gathering place of the pilgrims, I saw John Winthrop building himself a house just like the one he had left behind. He and all the others took this vast journey because of what they saw as religious repression, and also because the famous wool trade of this area had collapsed after centuries of prosperity. They set out for what they described as a 'renovated' England, secure in freedom, pure in religion. I have always liked that word 'renovated'. It tells us that the first English-Americans did not throw away their ancient culture, but made it good and serviceable once more.

And so in March 1630 the first great Puritan emigration from these parts began, the first ship the *Arbella* arriving in Massachusetts Bay in June. Two years later, in 1632, these East Anglian settlers decided that they must build a good school, which they named Newton after the village across the river from Wormingford – some of the men from our airfield would have cycled there, or borrowed a Jeep to visit the Saracen's Head and its formidable landlady Miss Glass. The settlers then thought that their school should have a more imposing name and so they changed it to Cambridge. And then, when one of its pupils died leaving it half his estate, they called it after him – Harvard. When I stayed at Harvard, I visited the nearby Fogg Museum where, on a wall all by himself, I saw a carved medieval angel from a Suffolk church looking lonely and far from home. It was from Harvard that Governor Winthrop's nephew George Downing graduated in 1642. He would later give his name to Downing Street.

During the last war we East Anglians made our connection with the Americans stationed here via the cinema. Never before or since had the film imagery of both our countries been more powerful. But today, Rogation, I see two processions in the Wormingford lanes. One of young men from the United States, off duty from fighting, wandering about, writing letters home, courting girls, going to dances, pubs, to houses where they were to be made at home, and the other of the Church going from cornfield to water, from water to orchards, from orchards to cottages, from cottages to graves, and asking all the way. 'Ask, and it shall be given you.' Ask in Latin is *Rogare*. Rogation, and while you are at it, see that the young know the village boundaries.

In life we sometimes ask more of each other than can be given. In life we ask much of God and he at times would seem to ask much of us. But here we, an unlikely meeting it would have appeared to our mutual ancestors, asking nothing more today than to be together in a building which was theirs long ago.

People have always returned to the battlefields of their youth, Thermopylae, Agincourt, Culloden, Nashville, the Somme, and now to Wormingford airfield to connect with an experience which contained both the best and the worst in human behaviour, and their part in it. They connect too with the dead who were young when they died. Few of the East Anglians who went away to North America in the seventeenth century came back, but they left their names and many of their homes behind. The church registers are full of their names, the neighbourhood filled with their beautiful cottages and farms. And the paths, could we but see them, are still marked out by their footsteps. Their skies remain and some of their trees are seeing yet another spring. And at this moment we are listening to the very words from the King James Bible which caused them to forsake everything they understood here for what they believed was a purer understanding of Christ. It was the most sacred thing in their luggage, the Scriptures, their only real treasure.

And then there was another connection between us here and the States. Flowers – plants. The British are garden-conscious to an astonishing degree. It was once said around here that you could neglect your wife in an English village, but never your garden. About the same time as the *Arbella* was sailing to Massachusetts, other ships were sailing back from the southern and eastern seaboards laden with plants which had been collected by the Tradescants, father and son, head gardeners to the King. Virginia Creeper, Tradescantia and a thousand other botanical species which crossed the Atlantic and 'took', as we say, in our soil. Young John Tradescant was so gripped as a collector that he was once seen carefully digging up a rare plant in the heat of battle, cutting it from the grass with his sword and tucking it in his pocket.

The word 'connect' does not appear in the Authorized Version of the Bible. The word there is 'join' and it is used many times. St Paul, a famous connector of persons, insists that 'we be perfectly joined together'. He is saying, 'Connect with those who love and serve Christ, connect with your past, connect with your present, connect with your real self.'

Here is a love letter from John Winthrop to his wife Margaret as he set sail for Massachusetts. She would follow. It is exquisite.

> Mine own, mine only, my best beloved. Methinks it is a very long time since I saw or heard of my beloved, and I miss already the sweet comfort of thy most desired presence, but the rich mercy and goodness of my God makes supply of all wants. He sweetens all conditions to us, he takes our cares and fears

from us. He will guide us in our pilgrimage. My dear wife, be of good courage: it shall go well with thee. Once again let us kiss and embrace. Your ever John Winthrop.

And it did go well with Mrs Winthrop, for a few months later she was safely across the Atlantic Ocean in the little wooden ship to become, one might say, the first First Lady – Margaret from Maplestead, Essex. Only connect.

Ascension

Time was when the village school all trooped to church on Ascension Day, sang all those thrilling Wesley Alleluias and was then released in a rush for play, for bike rides, for anything you liked. I had quite forgotten this when in my twenties, I woke up in the little town of Vézelay to – tumult! Bells were crashing, swallows were flying in and out of windows, people were pouring up the hill to the glorious church which crowned it, dogs were going mad, voices were raised. Why? What? '*L'Ascension!*' Of course, of course! In no time I was singing in the cool basilica, 'All praise to thee who art gone up', whilst outside on Vézelay's own height, far dizzier than our Mount Bures, the grapes felt the first hot sun.

'So then after the Lord had spoken unto them, he was received up into heaven, and sat on the right hand of God.' The last words of St Mark's Gospel.

'And he led them out as far as to Bethany, and he lifted up his hands and blessed them. And it came to pass, while he blessed them, he was parted from them, and carried up into heaven.' The last words of St Luke's Gospel.

*   *   *

'And when he had spoken these things, while they beheld, he was taken up and a cloud received him out of their sight.' The first words of Acts.

Clouds are used figuratively in the Bible – as they are by artists until the arrival of Constable, who used them meteorologically, being a miller's son. Until he painted them correctly, clouds simply reflected human moods. Black clouds whirled around warriors or the wicked, fleecy clouds floated across lovers, golden clouds glowed above the saints. But Constable saw them scientifically according to the weather and the time of day. In 1817 he had read the first textbook on meteorology to be published in Britain. It was Luke Howard's *The Climate of London*. It gave cloud formations names such as cirrus and cumulus. The first reference in Scripture to clouds as symbols of God's wrath or love is when, in Genesis, he tells Noah that he will use the rainbow to remind him of his promise not to destroy us. His 'bow shall be in the cloud'. Constable loved rainbows. He painted one across his 'Salisbury Cathedral' and another across his 'Stoke-by-Nayland Church'. Scientifically, seven colours, red, orange, yellow, green, blue, indigo and violet span the sky when the sun, at an attitude approximately of 42 degrees, shines through a rainstorm. At the same time, for this great artist, bow and cloud both hide and display a divine glory. Earth is connected to heaven, humanity to its everlasting home. 'My bow I set in the cloud.'

Quite the best description of the cloud which took the

risen Christ beyond human sight is by an unknown four-teenth-century writer.

> Do not think that because I call it a 'darkness' or a 'cloud' it is the sort of cloud you see in the sky, or the kind of darkness you know at home when the light is out. By 'darkness' I mean 'a lack of knowing', just as anything that you do not know, or may have forgotten may be said to be 'dark' to you, for you cannot see it with your inward eye. For this reason it is called a 'cloud', not of the sky, of course, but a cloud of unknowing between you and your God.

St Paul put it succinctly, telling us that now we see as through a glass, darkly, but then – face to face! Roman glass wasn't clear. One saw shadows through it.

But there was nothing shadowy about that last walk of Jesus and his disciples from Bethany, the village which had been his resting place in this world. It was during the familiar act of blessing that he parted from them, says Luke. 'He was lifted up and a cloud received him from their sight.' He whom they had watched and heard as a human being could no longer be seen. They had stared and stared until he was no longer physically visible. Did they mourn? Not a bit. They were happy and exhilarated. Old Ezekiel had spoken of a 'day of cloud, a day of reckoning', but that cloud which made it impossible for the Lord's companions to witness his homecoming wasn't a gloomy one.

Were we present and looking up on that first Ascension Day, our attention drawn to something beyond this world, and were we asked what we were seeing, we could answer, 'Christ's humanity – his human nature – taking its place with God'. Which means, of course, that there is room for our humanity in that same presence. I have always found ascension happiness different from resurrection happiness. The Paschal candle lit on Easter Day is extinguished on Ascension Day. I – all of us – stand where things are not so plainly seen. Long ago there were processions to mark Christ's last walk on earth when Psalm 8 was sung. 'What is man, that thou art mindful of him, and the son of man, that thou visitest him?' It is a song to the Creator of the universe which marvels at his interest in it. It was sung in May when the earth was at its most beautiful. There is no rejection of it in the Ascension story. Rather instead Christ carries with him into realms unknowable this side of heaven our appreciation of life here. We tell God how excellent his name is in all the world. And not only the world, but the cosmos, 'the works of his fingers' for we recognize his hand in everything.

In 1821 John Constable painted an 'Ascension' for the altarpiece of Manningtree church. After various vicissitudes it is at this moment (Ascension Day 2001) being placed over the north door of St Mary's Dedham. A local brewer, distantly related to the artist, had paid for it. It is the trans-figured-resurrected Jesus who rises, a physical being about to shed his earthliness, wonderful though it is, and to become what we here are unable to look at. Neither Constable's real weather clouds nor art's moody clouds are there to receive him from our sight. Only a sense of our being allowed to glimpse him at the penultimate moment of his earthly existence. Mr Alston the brewer commissioned it in the hope that it would put him on good terms with the Archdeacon of Colchester who controlled the licensing of the local pubs. What more earthbound motive for a soaring work of art could be found than this? Nor was Constable's own reaction to the commission any more high-minded. 'I must go into Suffolk soon on account of a *job*', he told his friend Archdeacon Fisher. Yet the ascending Christ is the first thing one sees on entering Dedham church, catching the eyes, holding the attention, making one think. As a pupil at Dr Grimwood's school, John Constable would have been marched into St Mary's on Ascension Day to sing those mysterious hymns, though less ecstatically than those I joined in in Vézelay, I suspect.

'Ye men of Galilee, why stand ye gazing up into heaven?'

Why, indeed.

The Great Lesson

---◆---

Now and then the service needs to be pulled up or slowed down, however perfectly sung or said. Or so we occasionally think. Familiarity is smudging its meaning. In his Sermon on the Mount Jesus is critical of public prayer – 'vain repetitions' – and his followers would have known only too well what he meant for they would have taken part in the beautiful liturgy of Temple and synagogue. They would also have seen the worship of Jove and Diana in the classical temples of Roman occupied Palestine. We now observe Muslim and Hindu prayer, and in our ignorance of these faiths it might well sound like 'babbling on'. And yet when Christ teaches his friends how to pray, he is in no way denying the validity of public prayer but is saying that it must contain the private element of each worshipper if it is to be more than sacred recitation.

One of the strangest requests in the Gospels must surely be that of the unnamed disciple who said to Jesus, 'Lord, teach us how to pray.' Like our Muslim neighbours, and not like most of us, his disciples had been brought up to observe a prayer-punctuated day. There was prayer at home, prayer at work, prayer at the synagogue and, on high days and holidays, prayer in King Herod's lovely new Temple.

Prayers which were never missed. They were as normal a part of life as getting up and going to bed. But on this occasion, writes Luke, 'as he was praying in a certain place, when he ceased', those who were watching him longed to pray like him. This was prayer as they had never before known it. It was then that he told them, 'When ye pray, say, Our Father which art in heaven . . .' Matthew sets the Lord's Prayer towards the end of the Sermon on the Mount, and after his fierce denunciation of showy religion. Instead, find some quiet spot and say, 'Our Father which art in heaven . . .' It is one of Christianity's profound moments. The prayer language is startling, its authority unchallengeable. Although, like anything else which is said over and over again, its edge can be blunted. I have always disliked the Church's sometime use of it as a mantra or a penance. Let us each hear it, if we can, as freshly as that handful of men heard it after its author had finished his own prayers. They had seen John the Baptist teach prayer to his followers, now Jesus must do the same.

Christ had been extracting religion from religious observance. Acts of kindness were not to be accompanied with the blare of trumpets. Attention was not to be drawn to oneself in the synagogue. Come closest to God in a quiet room, behind the locked door. If they enjoyed public worship, as we all do, with its singing and ritual, and the holy dream of its celebrations, the disciples could have felt rather crushed. The human warmth of faith in the ancient collective sense, and which we experience every Sunday, was being denied. Although of course what Jesus was teaching was that the completeness of one person's prayerfulness, when added to similar experiences of coming close to him in 'the quiet room' could but intensify what happens when we come to church.

There are two versions of the Lord's Prayer in the Gospels. Matthew's is the longer. We say it in William Tyndale's translation, words which have been so ground into Western civilization's prayerfulness that recent versions of them often act like variations to trip us up.

> Our Father, which art in heaven, hallowed be thy Name. Thy kingdom come. Thy will be done, in earth as it is heaven. Give us this day our daily bread. And forgive us our trespasses, as we forgive them that trespass against us. And lead us not into temptation, but deliver us from evil; for thine is the kingdom, the power, and the glory, for ever and ever, Amen.

The magnificent concluding doxology comes from the Scottish *Book of Common Prayer* published in 1637, and is not in the Bible.

Lent is as good a time as any to slow down the 'service' and to let the Lord's Prayer escape its ritual bonds. We repeat it twice at all three services, Matins, Evensong and Holy Communion, or rather where the latter is concerned, the priest first says it by himself and then we say it all together. In it we address God as our Father in heaven. This always reminds me, although I don't suppose it was meant to do so, that I had a father here on earth. We then ask God for four things. Fathers provide for their children. God is our ultimate provider, the source of all that we should need. And here are the four things which Christ tells us to ask God for:

> *Daily bread* – i.e. food. Not a month or a year's supply, but just enough to see us through the day. Jesus is the Master of Today-ness. Turn your back on the past. Do not think too much about the future. Live today.

> *Forgiveness.* God's forgiveness, our forgiveness.

> *Not to test us beyond our human individual strength.* This petition has often struck the Christian as strange. How unfair that God should lead us into temptation. But it is all about his knowing our strengths and weaknesses, and testing us accordingly.

> *Deliverance from evil.* Nothing ambiguous about this petition. How often have we not been held back by the good in us from what would be bad for us! From what would be bad for others too. Evil goes farther than 'sin'. We are inescapably sinners but rarely evil. We have been delivered from such a horrible fate. The petition should be accompanied by gratitude.

The Lord's Prayer is said in the plural. We are all in it together, this hungry, seeking, transgressing world. We ask God to feed it, and not just ourselves, to forgive it its greed and cruelties, its pride and materialism, to hold it back when it would go beyond its limits, to deliver it from its apparently limitless evil. A dozen men on a Palestinian hillside less than two thousand years ago, which is as nothing in universe-age time, were the first to hear it. Did they look at each other in surprise and say, 'So this is prayer!' Did Jesus himself pray it in the privacy of the guest room at Bethany?

It was of course the first prayer taught to Christian converts. At the early Eucharists it was said between the Breaking of Bread and the Kiss of Peace. It was believed that the apostles actually used it to consecrate the bread and wine. Prayer has two laws. It utters our belief in a transcendent yet personally present Jesus, and a belief in his kingdom of love. The Lord's Prayer is partly adoration – 'For thine is the kingdom, the power and the glory' – and partly one of childlike asking for the basic necessities for existing on the earth. It came out of Christ's homelessness and hunger, and out of what he saw during his wandering ministry.

There are two kinds of prayer, one on our tongues, the other in our heads. Vocal prayer, which is usually communal prayer, nearly always includes praise, thankfulness and penitence. Wordless prayer can go on all day long without our knowing it. Or its eloquence sweeps through us as we sit in the summer garden or swim in the summer sea. 'Something is happening to me today', we tell ourselves. The 'something' is God's attention.

How often did Jesus have to repeat his prayer before his friends knew it by heart? Did they all sit down on the grass and learn it by rote, like pupils in a Victorian village school? 'Our Father . . . hallowed be thy name . . . the power and the glory . . .' Amen!

Say 'Thank You'

---◆---

Gratitude can be politely automatic or it can be heartfelt. One of the first things I notice when I am in
America is the far fewer 'pleases' and 'thank yous'. It might
be historically due to the abolition of words belonging to
the old servitude. Yet, which I find dignified and attractive,
both young and old men will address each other as sir. The
central act of our worship has been called 'the Lord's Supper', 'Holy Communion', 'the Mass' and 'the Eucharist',
and it is by its last title that we address it at *Corpus Christi*
as we show our gratitude for the wonderfully imaginative
thought of Jesus in creating such a link between himself
and those who love him. The Last Supper was the first
Eucharist. Eucharist means thanksgiving. 'And when he had
given thanks . . .' Gratitude is at the heart of this feast and
at the heart of our faith. The psalms, the hymns, our public
and private prayer streams with it. 'Now thank we all, our
God, with hearts and hands and voices.' Note the order –
heartfelt thanks, practical thanks, musical and poetic thanks.

Corpus Christi makes me think of two grateful women,
one of whom I know about in a somewhat vague historical
fashion, the other a total stranger I had never heard of
until last Thursday (May 30th, 2000). One lived in Belgium

during the thirteenth century, one lives in Australia at this moment. One taught the Church to say thank you to Christ for instituting a service of communication between us for all time via the simple essentials of a meal, the other taught me how thankful I should be for the Gospel. Each of these teachers of gratitude stirred up what thankfulness I had in me and reminded me of all those times when I had not said 'Thank you' – at least, not with conviction. All of us, having had access to Christ's meal and Christ's words all our lives, tend to take them for granted, maybe. We have been well brought up, of course, and say grateful words as required, but without any deep feeling of having been given anything. The words are in the book, the food is on the altar, where they always are. 'Take ... eat ... drink...' 'What do you say?' our mothers used to remind us. We were being taught good manners rather than gratitude. But gifts such as the Eucharist and the Gospel cannot be accepted with merely good manners.

This was why the first of my grateful women, after much persuasion, got the Church to set aside a day of intense gratitude on which Jesus could be truly thanked for what he called his 'Memorial'. This grateful woman's name was Juliana and she was the rather trying mother superior of a convent near Liège. So trying indeed was Juliana that they forced her to leave. Saints can be a great nuisance at times. All the same, she fought her corner, as we say, and she also acquired formidable support for her views, and in the year 1246 she got her way. The first feast of *Corpus Christi* was celebrated. *Corpus Christi* – 'Take, eat, this is my Body which is given for you. Do this in remembrance of me.' Juliana was fifty-four years old. Alas, it would be the only celebration of thanksgiving for the Holy Communion in her lifetime and she herself would suffer exile from her community until her death. But only six years later her feast of gratitude was officially sanctioned by the Church, and here on this summery Thursday evening we too concentrate on our gratitude for the Eucharist.

There are just a handful of us. Last Sunday at Little Horkesley at the Deanery Service we 'filled the temple like the Lord's train' in Isaiah's vision, and now we have those 'two or three gathered together in my name', which Jesus loved and recognized as a perfect congregation. Both group-ings are inspiring, both necessary, both are thankful. No one really knows why Juliana was so unpopular in her convent. Perhaps she was bossy. Or ambitious and wanted to make her mark. Perhaps her nuns thought that they thanked God quite enough when they received Holy Com-munion and did not see any reason to have a separate big thank you for it. They must have been a tough bunch to have ousted such a mother superior. But Juliana won in the end, which is why we are here on the Thursday after Pentecost, and why most of Europe is on holiday. 'He took bread, *and when he had given thanks*, he broke it, and gave it to his disciples.'

But what of the other grateful woman? Who is she? No one in the world at large would have heard of her until, this Corpus Christi morning, her Australian voice gave 'Prayer for Today' on the radio. But what a voice! So true, so unforgettable. I never caught the name, I caught the voice. In the brief space allowed for this programme it seemed to cover all human time and fill it with a gratitude which was quite unimaginable to someone like myself. Perhaps you listened to it. The speaker was an elderly aborigine. As she told the world about her life she could, with all justice, have turned on her Australian background and said, 'Thanks for nothing!' For she and her race had been treated abominably. My first sight of aborigines was in a small New South Wales timber town called Grafton. They were a group of unemployed young men sitting by the side of a dusty hot road drinking beer from cans. They looked defeated. But later on I was taken by my nephew to a height overlooking the Pacific Ocean where I could see other aborigine young people swimming. This height was a 'dreaming place', one of those quiet locations where for thousands of years the native people of Australia would rest and contemplate, and discover their spiritual strength. There were Stone Age-like carvings, and a hollow in a rock where a dreaming man could fit his hip. There was a huge sky and arum lilies growing like docks grow at home.

When Jesus spent a month in the wilderness it was a nightmare. The loneliness, the hunger, the cold, the hallucinations. For aborigines their month dreaming is a kind of first step to paradise. Nature heals them, the earth restores them. They become whole or holy. I sat on the warm carvings listening to the far cries from the beach and thought how advanced the aboriginal spirituality was compared to that of the 'Christianity' which repressed it.

The *Corpus Christi* speaker on 'Prayer for Today' had been the product of a raped native woman and a white settler. She and her brothers and sisters had been taken from their home and placed in state care, to be brought up 'civilized'. But now she uses the site of her mother's house as a kind of dream place where she not only thanks God for the plants which grow there, the animals and birds, but also for the Gospel of Christ. She said that in spite of what had been taken from her by white men, they had given her the Gospel. So she gave thanks for the gospel. She said that she had added the Gospel of Christ to her ancient religion. She said that because it was the custom of her people to conceive on the bare earth, she had chosen as her 'Prayer for Today' a verse from Genesis. 'Then the Lord God formed a man from the dust of the ground and breathed into his nostrils the breath of life. Thus the man became a living creature.'

And so we have on the Feast of *Corpus Christi*, the woman who invented it as a day of gratitude, and the woman who had everything taken from her and had nothing to be grateful for. Except, as a matter of official policy, she had been given something which gradually filled the space of all her deprivations – the Gospel. St Paul told her that it would make her free, and it had. Free from anger, free from what had happened to her.

The feast days of the Church exist to jog our memory and play-up our imagination. Juliana from Liège and the lady from Australia would each have been reassured by St John when he wrote:

> But we belong to God ... Dear friends, let us love one another, because love is from God. Every one who loves is a child of God, and knows God.
>
> (1 John 4.6–7 NEB)

The Turncoats

It is midsummer and I find myself thinking of two men whose lives changed direction in a flash. It often happens. We jog along in the usual way and then something occurs which entirely re-routes us, as it were. Although unsettling, there is no going back. I am reminding myself of two men in particular who had to do some quick thinking during a moment of crisis in their lives and to take a path which must inevitably lead to their deaths. But equally, it led to their immortality – although neither of them at that second of decision had this reward in mind. Their names were Saul and Alban, and they lived nearly three hundred years apart, one in Palestine, one in Britain.

Saul had set off to Damascus to arrest its heretics, his pocket full of warrants, and had returned to Jerusalem a heretic – that is, a Christian – himself. And calling himself Paul. No wonder he was received with two kinds of fear, that of Christ's friends who knew his ruthlessness of old, and that of those who had sent him to Damascus, knowing that if any one could rid the city of this dangerous sect, he could. Saul was the man when you wanted the law applied. But here he was, come home as advocate for this splinter group with its erroneous belief that the Messiah had come

– and had been killed. All this had to be nipped in the bud, and Saul could have done it, but he had been re-routed. How? What had changed his thinking? And so suddenly?

It took the apostles a lot of convincing that Saul, sorry, Paul, was now an apostle too. They were remembering his role, a despicable one, when poor young Stephen was stoned to death for blasphemy, how Saul had stood there guarding the coats. How could they forget it? How could Paul forget it? He never could. The terrible things he had done before he was re-routed at the very gates of Damascus troubled him for the rest of his days. All he could say was, 'I am what I am, a bad man redeemed by Christ.' To the authorities he was no more than a turncoat and they set out to get him. Their opportunity arrived when he was seen breaking the law by taking a Greek into the Temple. This man's name was Trophimus and he came from Ephesus. It was sacrilege for a non-Jew to enter the Temple. There was the usual uproar, the waving of fists and shouting. 'Some cried one thing, some another.' Paul was arrested, beaten and chained. The mob itself was so large that it swept the prisoner and his guard along with it. They managed to escape further mob violence by taking refuge in a fort.

I remember watching on television the Swedish police being chased by a furious crowd. It was in Gothenberg and along a street which I had once walked, and so I felt vaguely connected with the drama. But it brought to mind Paul and his near-destruction by a raging crowd. The captain of the guard was angry with his prisoner for having caused this popular uprising. But Paul told the captain who he was, no rabble-rouser but 'a Jew from Tarsus, a city in Cilicia, a citizen of no mean city, so let me speak to the crowd'. He then stood on the stairs and addressed the crowd in Hebrew. Hearing him speak in their own tongue quietened the people down. Paul was open with them. He told them that he had gone to school in Tarsus and that his teacher's name was Gamaliel the famous Jewish rabbi. But when he went on to say what had happened to him on the road to Damascus, they refused to believe a word of it. They threw off their clothes, threw dust in the air and went mad. The captain then thought that he would get at the real truth of the matter by scourging his troublesome prisoner. But Paul, of course, knew the law. A man could not be scourged until he had received a court sentence. We are reminded of the 'correct' scourging of Jesus, who had been sentenced to death. The captain then realized that Paul was a Roman, and what was more a born Roman. The captain shook. He had treated a Roman like a non-Roman, had bound him with chains, had attempted to scourge him. He told Paul the sad story of his struggle to get together enough money to purchase his own freedom, for he had been a slave, and all that it had cost him to be a Roman. Paul told him simply, 'I was born free.' His ministry would be all about setting the prisoner free.

Wisely, the captain took his prisoner to a Jewish court for trial, and there was a scene which was dangerously similar to that of the trial of Jesus, with the Roman authority washing its hands of the whole business, for it could make neither head nor tail of this strange people the Jews, with their religious law and their insistence on there being only one God. Whoever heard of there being a single God! Gods were everywhere, on mountain tops, down by the river, under the sea. Paul's God advised him to take his case to Rome itself. The Jews' God told them to assassinate him for being a blasphemer. And so the great apostle of Christ began his long litigious journey to the city where he believed he would receive true justice. The court scenes and Paul's eloquence make dramatic reading. 'Almost thou persuadest me to be a Christian,' sighed one of his judges.

A great many wonderful things happened before Paul received 'justice'. The respect due to a Roman may have accompanied him most of the way but it could not save him from his execution. That turning from Caesar to a greater authority, and all in a blinding flash of redirection, did for Saul in earthly terms. Who knows what he might have become had he not suddenly changed masters.

And it is at this point that we arrive at another parting of the ways, that of Alban, the British saint who shares the midsummer sun and equinox with John the Baptist. We know him better than most due to his quiet occupation of the right hand pedestal of our reredos here at Wormingford. There he is, the curly-headed proto-martyr of Britain as the Victorian sculpter imagined him, who did what Sydney Carton did for Evrémonde, swap clothes and die in place of an innocent victim of the law. Alban's friend was a priest who had told him about Christ who had said, 'Greater love has no man than he who gives his life for a friend.' It was round about AD 304 in what would one day be Hertfordshire, a place named after a ford where stags crossed a river. 'As pants the hart for cooling streams.' Although dressed in a priest's cowl, they soon found out that Alban was no more than a convert of 'a sacrilegious rebel'. He was commanded to worship the local gods. Like Jesus – and Paul eventually – they scourged him and then took him up a flowery hill and beheaded him. There was a huge crowd from nearby Verulamium to watch him die. Centuries later they built St Alban's Cathedral where he suffered.

I suspect that Alban did not work out some long-term plan to save his teacher's life. More likely, hearing the soldiers combing the huts for a Christian priest rumoured to be living there, and getting dangerously close, he would have grabbed the tell-tale robe and whispered, 'Run'. History allows us to use our imagination. Holy myths and fables were to crowd that flowery hilltop. A magnificent medieval shrine would crown it. But rising high above this human response to an impetuous act, this man's giving his life to save that of his friend, is the non-miraculous goodness of Alban. Legend would well-nigh smother it, but only for a time. We see the saint clearly these days. We might even wonder why he is not the patron saint of England. Not that anyone can make Alban more than he was, or is.

Paul and Alban, both citizens of no mean city, the City of God, who were re-routed to it. You may think that it was a very long time ago, but Roman bricks hold our church tower together and they could easily have been made by someone who saw an execution on Verulamium hill. The readings for St Alban's day are from Paul's letters to Timothy, those of a teacher to his pupil.

Cousin of the Lord

———◆———

A n ancient Advent hymn is realistic. A herald voice is
calling 'Christ is nigh' but the world can't quite hear
what is being said at first. Then the words break into its
consciousness with terrible force as they shake the cosmos.
'Cast away the dreams of darkness, O ye children of the
day!'

Jesus's own life apart, there is no more urgent existence
in the Gospels than that of his cousin John. It is a life which
edges along that mysterious perimeter between the physical
and the non-physical, and which presents human experience at its simplest, at its purest and at its most single-
minded. Also at its least self-concerned. From childhood
on, this son of an elderly clergyman and his far from young
wife, both of whom had long given up all hope of becoming
parents, knew what he had to do. Understood why he had
been born. It was to map out a path along which his country
could walk once more to God. Long ago this path was plain
to see and much travelled, but for generations now it had
been either forgotten or avoided and was now overgrown
and hard to find. The great prophet Isaiah's path obliterated
– never walked – it was incredible! That 'broad highway'
lost! In Isaiah's book John had read:

'The voice said, Cry.'
'What shall I cry? All flesh is grass, and all the goodliness thereof is as the flower of the field . . . The grass withereth, the flower fadeth, but the word of our God shall stand for ever.'   (Isa. 40.6–8 KJV)

The prophet becomes insistent and tells John, 'Lift up your voice and shout! Lift it up fearlessly and cry, "Your God is here!"' This wild and thrilling command made by Isaiah hundreds of years ago was to dominate John's short life. To prepare himself for heraldry he remained celibate and kept himself going with only the barest necessities, living in the open air and waiting for that end-of-Advent-day when he could run down to the old sacred river of his little country and cry, 'Your God is here!'

When eventually he did so, everyone was intrigued. They saw a familiar figure who reminded them of somebody else. The priests were worried and sent a deputation to ask him who he really was. Knowing what was in their minds he said, 'I am not the Messiah.' The deputation was relieved. Crazy, holy young men were often tempted to set themselves up as saviours. There being a popular belief in the return of national heroes, they asked, 'What then – are you Elijah?' And when he shook his head they asked, 'Well then, are you the prophet we await?' 'No', said John. 'Then who are you? We must return with an answer. What account do you give of yourself?' And then came his great moment, that moment for which he had prepared himself all his young life.

I am a voice crying aloud in the wilderness, 'Make the Lord's highway straight!'

The deputation would have recognized the quotation. However as John was only another one of these ascetics, why was he baptizing people in the Jordan? Admittedly this purification ritual had not been practised for generations, but who gave him permission to revive it? These religious fanatics thought they could do what they liked. Where were this one's credentials? John's reply disturbed them. He told the deputation, 'I am nobody. I baptize with water but the person whose herald I am has the power to baptize you with his Holy Spirit. Why, I am not fit to undo his shoes!' This was said at Bethany. Nearby would have been that hospitable house where the tired Christ would rest after preaching along the dirty roads, and where the job of the lowest servant would have been to kneel before any guest, take off his sandals and wash the dust from his feet.

The day following John's protestation of his unworthiness to do even this for Jesus, he was by the river when he saw his Lord striding towards him. Turning to the crowd he said those words which have become immortalized in the *Agnus Dei*. 'Look, there is the Lamb of God who takes away the sin of the world!'

John had by this time his own group of followers – disciples – a fact which worried him. People should not attach themselves to heralds. One of his disciples was named Andrew. As Jesus passed by, John told his followers, '*There* is the Lamb of God!' Why 'lamb'? Because a sacrificial lamb had allowed the Jewish nation to come close to God from time immemorial. John was saying, 'Here is someone who will give you access to God!' John invented the title of 'Lamb of God' for Christ and used it often. Later on, another John would have a vision of heaven as he toiled as a convict in a saltmine on a remote island. Looking up, he would see, 'A Lamb with the marks of slaughter on him standing at the right hand of God', and would hear the voices of God's messengers singing, 'Worthy is the Lamb to receive all power, wisdom, honour, glory and praise!' (Rev. 5.12).

John the Baptist's cousinship with Jesus was a favourite subject for the old Italian and Spanish artists. They liked to paint a family portrait of Mary and Joseph and two small boys, one on the Virgin's lap, one clinging to her knee. They were born six months apart, John in the Judean hills, Jesus in the town of his ancestors a few miles south of Jerusalem. The old artists also liked to paint the 'Salutation' when Mary climbed the hill to tell her cousin Elizabeth that she too was pregnant. The warm-hearted southern Europeans, family-loving people, delighted in these natural relationships. It was exactly what their own mothers would have done. It was to Elizabeth that Mary, in the joyous Jewish way, sang her thanksgiving song the *Magnificat*. And it was to his wife and the neighbours that John's father sang his thanksgiving song which we call *Benedictus*. We see our liturgy bursting, as it were, from the thankfulness of these two families.

Jesus was just beginning his ministry when he heard of his cousin's horrible death. The shock was appalling. Matthew says, 'He withdrew privately by boat to a lonely place' in which to mourn his herald. When we contemplate the sufferings of Christ we tend not to include this tragic moment. But it was the Lord's greatest bereavement on this earth, the loss of John. When he found the lonely place he wept.

It is part of our faith to know that its founder and his herald lived and taught in an ordinary place – a native place for both of them. At midsummer St John's Wort will be in bloom under my baytree. *Hypericum perforatum.* It was a magic plant for our ancestors. They smoked it over bonfires and used it as medicine. It was golden and fretted like the midsummer sun and it reminded them of Jesus's enchanting description of his dear cousin, 'He was light – a burning and a shining light!' They believed it was a flower which contained an extra dose of the sun. But it is in winter that:

> On Jordan's bank the Baptist's cry
> Announces that the Lord is nigh.

Looking Seawards

---◆---

O n St Peter's day we must turn to the shore-line. The sea creates a special kind of person. There are landsmen and seamen. The latter are now not only fishermen and sailors but oilmen on their hazardous rigs, environmentalists on their equally hazardous ship *Green Peace*, and archaeologists searching for drowned cities. Even in these days of air travel, we have only to drive to a port or have a holiday in the midst of coast-dwellers, to realize that the sea, like the past, is a foreign country where they do things differently. Anyone who has anything to do with it, whether a boy playing on the beach or a crew sailing a yacht, or a passenger on a cross-Channel ferry, all comparatively safe occupations compared with those long voyages of only a few years ago, feels its unreduced power. The sea is beautiful but terrifyingly beautiful. Its immensity alone seems to drown our thoughts and standards.

The New Testament is dominated by two seas, the Sea of Galilee, which is a large freshwater lake some eighteen miles long and eight miles wide, and the Mediterranean. Galilee was notorious for its sudden squalls which blew up without warning. Until I recognized how devastating these brief, wild storms could be, I tended rather to despise the disciples for becoming hysterical on that famous occasion when Jesus, dog-tired after teaching all day, fell asleep just when Galilee became turbulent. I also forgot that fishermen did not learn to swim. Throughout marine history men who go down to the sea purposely were unable to swim, and why? Because it would make death by drowning a long struggle. Nelson couldn't swim. When Peter, losing faith as he imitated Christ's walk on water, began to sink, he shouted in panic, 'Save me!' Had he been able to swim he would have struck out for his fishing boat so near at hand.

Frequently the life of Jesus is shown to us as an inlander's life, with its constant references to cornfields, hills, vineyards and urban centres. But it was an inland which could never be far from the sea and most of his followers were shoremen and people who had made voyages. Mary Magdalen came from the seaside village of Magdala. The Romans he met had sailed the Mediterranean – or possibly what is now the North Sea. Shipping and sea merchandise were everywhere. 'Greeks', that is non-Jews, were everywhere with their tales from across the sea. News of the whole world would have sailed in to Palestine. The very freshness of his teachings has something of the illimitable nature of the oceans about them, and he liked the nature of salt, how it brought a flavour to life. He said that a bland existence, one without an exciting commitment to God, was no life at all. His followers would liven up the human condition and make the journey from this earth to 'the kingdom' wonderful.

The most ill-founded description we have of the disciples

Boats

is that they were 'simple' fishermen. Fishermen the chief followers of Christ decidedly were, simple they were not. Had they been the clumsy, ignorant men of legend, Jesus would not have had such a difficult time with them. He would have led, they would have followed, he the Good Shepherd, they the good sheep. But sheep-like is exactly not what Peter and the others were. They followed their Lord, certainly, but argumentatively, questioningly, and with often pertinent demands as to where he was taking them. They showed that they had minds of their own and tongues of their own.

The four fishermen, Simon and his brother Andrew and James and his brother John were all recruited by Jesus on the same day. It was, 'Do not say goodbye, do not make any arrangements. Drop everything and follow me.' Considering how cantankerous they could be, it was proof of his sublime authority that they did just that – walking away from all they understood, families, trade, routine, religious conventions, and from the lapping shore which had been their background since birth. And walking into a new law which was thrilling, compelling – and dangerous. There being something firm and monumental about Simon, Jesus nicknamed him Peter – Rock – and what there was about the brothers James and John to receive the nickname 'Sons of Thunder' we can only guess. Andrew remained Andrew. The Sons of Thunder clearly had not got Christ's message when they wanted to set fire to a village which had been unwelcoming. Neither had their mother when she wanted

Jesus to give her sons the best places at high table when he came into his kingdom. Jesus wasn't angry with her, simply telling her that she didn't know what she was asking. Could she or anyone 'Drink my cup'?

Christ saw his fishermen, not as simple adults but as men at the infancy of their faith. For a long time they saw him as a successor to some earthly throne, even that of Caesar himself. A little king, Herod Agrippa, would soon behead poor James. Small men in power never put up with sons of thunder. St James was the first of the Lord's friends to be executed, following the death of his cousin John. It showed the peril they were all in. Everything would have changed at this moment, the carefree abandonment of the old life, the learning about the new life. Another authority had its eye on them. It required courage to follow Jesus. Their families would have been pleading, 'Come home!' Who knows? If the tale can be believed, James, Son of Thunder was to end up in a glorious silver box at Compostella after his body was cast up on the Spanish shore, to be wondered at by pilgrims to this day. Of all the four fishermen, his was to be the most glittering fate – in this world, anyway. He was like a silver fish himself, swimming mystically those seas which, when alive, he was unable to swim physically, then captured in a shrine. It does one good to give up everything for a couple of weeks and walk to see him, as thousands still do.

Matthew the ex-taxman tells us that his brother disciples occasionally got fed up with James and John. Once when the wrangling was particularly bad, Jesus called all his disciples together and was severe with them. They must not confuse this authority with that of the authorities in Jerusalem – or at Rome, if it came to that. And then he did an astonishing thing. He singled out a fisherman to be the foundation on which he would build the Church. 'Thou art Peter, and upon this rock' – and here we can imagine him taking the amazed disciple by the hand – 'I will build my Church, and the gates of hell shall not prevail against it. And I will give thee the keys of the kingdom.'

Did the others say, '*Simon*. Why him? Why not one of us?' I think not. By this time everyone near to Christ would have seen something in Peter, and in Jesus's attitude towards him, which revealed some kind of pre-eminence in him, some kind of reliability about him. What happened after the sentencing of Christ had more to do with Peter's humanity than with his unreliability. The Church was built up on a vulnerable man and not on some super-hero.

The fishermen James, John, Simon and Andrew have a kind of primacy among the Twelve which is hard to explain. In a sense they *do* sit on the Lord's right and left hands in our concept of them. It was they who were present when he was transfigured and when he prayed at Gethsemane, the height and depth of his earthly emotion. On neither occasion were they able to comprehend the height and depth of what was happening to their Master. How could they? They were still only disciples – learners. But soon they would receive their commissions and be apostles. The sea of faith with its depths and storms and wide opportunities would be roaring in their ears, and the Church itself would become a ship of souls keeping Christ's words afloat.

Exporting the Word

P art-way through Pentecost we come to one of the best descriptions of an ancient sea voyage ever written. It closes that great travel book which we call the Acts of the Apostles. Acts – movement. The infant Church was lacking in movement, was holed up in secret rooms and uncertain as to what to do or where to go. And it was guilty about this, for had not the last words of its founder been that unequivocal directive, 'Go out into all the world and preach the gospel'? But how? It seemed an impossible task. 'All the world' – when all that his followers knew was a little land about the size of Wales. *All* the world was the Roman Empire, an immense territory spread around the middle sea. How on earth were they to cross the Mediterranean, or walk through many foreign countries to Rome itself? The dangers were legendary. Yet, the Lord's command was unambiguous. 'Go out into all the world and teach others what I have taught you.'

His last apostle, although someone who flinched from calling himself one, Paul, seemed to have been a born travel-ler. He had what we would call an international outlook, perhaps because he had been brought up on a trading route and was also the proud possessor of a dual nationality which gave him confidence, being both Roman and a Jew. He could go anywhere. In fact it was Paul's over-confidence in the fairness of Roman justice which initiated his famous voyage to what he called 'no mean city', Rome itself, and to his execution. Unlike Peter and the others, he had always been a man of the world. He had seen its great places. They had been nowhere. Just up and down Judea, to Jerusalem at festival time, to the familiar Galilean beaches for their fishing boats, to the wild heights above. But they did have one huge advantage over Paul because all these simple walks had been in the company of Christ himself.

Paul knew men who travelled far and wide on big ships, the masters of vessels and superstitious sailors. But such men did not know him. They thought him unusual and strange, and didn't want him aboard. He was a man who gave orders, who took over, who would certainly bring bad luck. They were full of misgivings when he came aboard and comforted themselves with the secret decision that should he endanger the ship he could be shoved into the sea. It was possible that when Paul opted for a trial in Rome instead of in Caesarea, he had not given much thought as to how he would get there. Of course, passenger and cargo ships plied regularly to and from all the many ports of the empire, some often carrying important prisoners. Paul appears to have underestimated his position as a prisoner-passenger, as well as the impression he made on ordinary people. He had taken a fatal step when he opted to be tried in Rome. Had he not done so, King Agrippa would have released him, and the entire history of the Church would have been different. But Paul would have been thinking of another trial, and that not so long ago, when a judge had found no fault with the prisoner and washed his hands of the case, for outside the courtroom there was baying for Paul's blood. Who could protect him from a fate like that of his Master? So to Rome it was. Paul would be tried as a Roman, not as a Jew. It was his prerogative.

Naval historians like to study Paul's long voyage to Italy because of all its circumstantial detail. This is so vivid that the reader can sniff the salty air, smell Africa on the wind, as one does now in part of the Mediterranean, and hear the rigging cracking and the seabirds shrieking. His ship was to carry him to Puteoli on the west coast of Italy, from whence he would walk the forty miles along the Appian Way to the capital. Strangely, though filled with near-disasters, it proved to be the apostle's easiest journey. His travels over-land had met with every hardship and difficulty imaginable, and he had once, in rage, poured these out to those who accused him of gadding about all over the place, instead of attending to matters at home.

But there was another reason for making this trip, one which went far beyond the claims of earthly citizenship. One night in Caesarea a voice had whispered in his ear, 'Keep up your courage. You have affirmed me in Jerusalem; you must do the same in Rome.' This was the real reason why he was going. Paul was not the only prisoner aboard but one of a group. They were all under the guard of a

Looking towards the Wash

centurian of the Augustan Cohort, no less, a man named Julius, an officer of the Emperor's own regiment. Paul impressed Julius so much that when the ship docked at Sidon, where Paul had friends, he allowed him to stay with them. Sidon was an industrial port full of metalworkers. In the light of what was to come, one wonders if the ship was overladen with heavy goods. No sooner had it sailed than head winds forced it to sail under the lee of Cyprus and not take to the open sea. When it reached Myra, all the prisoners except Paul were transferred to another vessel.

The head winds did not abate. In fact they grew worse after this and the ship continued to creep along by the coast, this time near Crete. It was all, to use one of Paul's favourite words, perilous. This part of the Aegean had always been a ships' graveyard. They struggled on to a place called Fair Havens where Paul could see at once the dangers of continuing their journey. He advised the crew as much. 'I can see, gentlemen, that this voyage will be disastrous. It will mean great loss. Loss not only of the ship and cargo but also loss of life.' There were two hundred and seventy-six people aboard, 'souls', as they were known to sailors. But neither the captain nor the centurian listened to their extraordinary prisoner. They made a run for a Cretan harbour named Phoenix, hugging the coast all the way. When a north-easterly wind caught them, they could do no more than allow it to drive the ship as it willed, and after they had thrown much of its tackle overboard. It is at this point on his wild journey that St Paul begins to sound like Conrad. They were forced to drag the dinghy on deck to prevent it being washed away. Their helplessness became the helplessness of *The Ancient Mariner* – 'And when neither sun nor stars in many days appeared, and no small tempest lay on us, all hope that we should be saved was then taken away.'

It was at this point that Paul's authority was recognized. He began to take over, to comfort, to reassure. 'Now I urge you not to lose heart. Not a single life will be lost – only the ship.' A statement which would not have comforted its owner, who was aboard. Fourteen days later they were still adrift and the crew tried to abandon ship, lowering the dinghy and pretending that they were going to lay out anchors from the bows. It was Paul and his guard Julian who soon put a stop to this mutiny by slashing the ropes which held the dinghy and letting it fall into the sea. The following day, the fifteenth of the voyage, Paul was telling the terrified souls that not a hair of their heads would be lost. He arranged a meal and said grace. We might stretch our theology and claim that this was the first Eucharist to have been celebrated at sea. After this meal they further lightened the ship by throwing its wheat store into the waves. The next morning an early sun showed them land – a nearby shore with a creek. It was with immense relief that they ran the ship aground. They had come to Malta. St Paul and Christianity had set foot in Europe.

The Maltese, whom St Paul called 'round islanders' treated these castaways with 'uncommon kindness', and because it was pouring with rain and they were all soaked, lit a bonfire, the apostle himself gathering sticks to make it blaze. And accidentally also picking up a snake, and shaking it off into the fire, poor creature, a presence of mind which decided the Maltese to declare him a god. More deserving of their praise was his curing them of their many complaints.

Three months later they were picked up by a ship named the *Castor and Pollux* which had been wintering in Malta. It was named after twins who had long been the guardians of navigators. A beautiful south wind blew them to Italy. They landed, after only three days at sea, at Puteoli, a delightful city full of wells and shipping, and from there Paul walked to Rome in the company of friends who had arrived to meet him. He rented a house in Rome and with a single guard to protect him began his great mission. 'First Jerusalem, then Rome.' 'He had stayed there two full years at his own expense, with a welcome for all who came to him,' writes St Luke, the author of Acts, 'proclaiming the kingdom of God [here lay the quarrel with Caesar], and teaching the facts about the Lord Jesus Christ, quite openly and without hindrance.'

Scholars have described St Paul as 'the most powerful personality in the history of the Church'. No one, then or later, would so brilliantly and totally carry the Gospel 'into all the world'. His teachings were a threat to the state. So they took him to the bank of the Tiber and executed him. But his commanding voice continued to be heard in his letters and his adventurous nature felt to this day. 'First Jerusalem, then Rome', and those dangerous seas which lay between, seas of religious and political repression on which it took a brave soul to chart another direction.

The Desires and Petitions of Thy Servants

————◆————

Every service contains prayers called petitions. Petition is a pleading, legal word. We petition God to help the hungry, the bereaved, the government, the prisoners, every individual and situation which can make a comprehensive and representative list for him to cast his loving eye over, and forgetting that he has the difficulties and miseries of the world always in his mind. In fact the prayerful tradition of asking him for assistance is really to remind ourselves of his knowledge of our needs. The great merit of congregational petitions is that they take us out of ourselves, as it were. We become powerfully concerned with others. It is not I but the Church itself asking God to help someone who could be in despair of his own voice ever being heard, and thus we become advocates for those unable to pray.

Few individuals are more collectively prayed for than hostages. A hostage is a pawn, in our day a person who is caught up in a medieval situation, their plight being all the more terrible for him because of this. A youngster goes back-packing and, unbelievably, he walks into a long-distant century. He is the innocent victim of a politics of which he knows nothing. He has been captured like a valuable bird and put in a cage – and less than a week ago he was beginning a holiday at Heathrow, and in less than a week to come he could be decapitated. Nothing can be done except to petition God, governments, his captors. Unbeknown to him, no sooner has his ransom been made public than he could be the object of half the world's love and concern, so barbaric is the fate which has befallen him. Petitioning, even on this scale, does not necessarily make itself heard to the person whose life may depend on its success. Terry Waite said that not a scrap of that warmth for him which was such a strong part of the petitionary prayers of churches everywhere during the years when he was chained up was felt by him. What kept him 'warm', as it were, was what he remembered in the Bible and Prayer Book, in hymns, in poems, in many wonderful fragments of written Christianity, some learned by rote in childhood. When at last he was freed he was astonished to discover the extent of the Church's petition for his safety. God's answer to it could have been this literary one, this saving the prisoner by what he held in his head from what he had sung and said a thousand times.

I shall never forget the astonishing press conference which Brian Keenan held in Dublin Castle after his release. There he was, a young man in a T-shirt seated before a bank of cameras in a magnificent stateroom after years of being chained to a wall in a filthy, cold Lebanese cell. Churches everywhere had been praying for him, kept up to the mark by his heroic girlfriend. The whole of Ireland, north and south, had sunk their differences, it seemed, in their petitionary fervour for his safety. And yet he was now making his extraordinary appearance with only the faintest notion of what a hostage is. The world, watching him and listening to him, expected him to say a few words about being free at last and how thankful he was for our prayers. Instead, in a shocked silence, he addressed the massed microphones in the language of Job:

> Hostage is the humiliating slipping away of every sense and fibre of body and mind and spirit that makes us what we are. Hostage is a mutant creation filled with fear, self-loathing, guilt and death-wishing. *But he is a man*, a rare, unique and beautiful creation of which these things are no part.

Then, speaking of his friendship with John McCarthy, Keenan continued,

> *His* abundant love of life suffered, as with all of us, a terrible and awful diminution, and those moments of hopelessness were a grinding of mind and heart. Yet, as I know from vast experience, where a man can find a will equal to vision and, *by force of the fire that is in him*, fuse these things, he is *undiminished*, and can never be diminished.

And he quotes John Milton's words from *Paradise Lost*: 'The mind is its own place, and in itself can make a heaven of hell, a hell of heaven.'

There was much more – more in a language which we do not expect to hear these days but which, once heard, plays havoc with our complacency – our kindly formal petitioning, if you like. I was reminded of a passage in St Luke's Gospel where Jesus reads the lesson for the first time in his local synagogue. The young speaker – well, thirty years old, which was rather late to be making such a debut – had recently returned from making a harsh retreat in the desert where he had certainly suffered an upsetting diminution of who he really was, and where he had certainly felt his spirit being degraded. But also where he had discovered 'a will equal to his vision' and thus, so strengthened, he had come through.

And here we have him home again on a Sabbath day and apparently safe among those he has known all his life. Here before him, as he stands up, is conventional religious order and a flurry of happy interest and expectation. Nazareth may have bred an orator, or even a prophet, and it felt happy that at last this familiar man was about to open his mouth. Luke writes:

> He came to Nazareth, where he had been brought up, and went to synagogue on the Sabbath day as he regularly did, and he stood up to read the lesson, and was handed the scroll of the prophet Isaiah. He opened the scroll and found the passage and read,
>
> 'The spirit of the Lord is upon me, because he has anointed me. He has sent me to announce good news to the poor, and *to proclaim release for prisoners*, and

recovery of sight for the blind; *to let the broken victims go free.'* (Luke 4.16–18 NEB)

Then, continues Luke, 'he rolled up the scroll, gave it back to the attendant, and sat down, and all eyes in the synagogue were fixed on him.' And thus Christ preached the one and only sermon on his home ground. Preached it to those who had known him, and yet not known him, all his life. Perhaps his own family was present. Certainly all the neighbours were because they said, 'Fancy Joseph the carpenter's son being able to preach like this. Such words, such thought. Wait until those intellectuals up in the Temple hear about him! He will put our synagogue on the map!' At first they loved what they heard. But then the carpenter's son began to get personal. He reminded the Nazarenes of their long history of intolerance. How they only liked to hear what made them feel good, and not those truths which alone can support a people during the crises of their history. No doubt, added Jesus, you will retort, 'Physician, heal thyself before you come to us with your remedies for a healthy society.' And he reminded them of their rejection of many of the great teachers God had sent them in the past, adding mordantly, that a prophet is not without honour except in his own country.

I was struck by the powerful use made by Brian Keenan of Isaiah's words – those same words which opened the ministry of Jesus: 'God has called me to open the blind eyes, to bring out the prisoners from the prison, and them that sit in darkness out of the prison house. I am the Lord: that is my name ... Sing unto the Lord a new song!' (Isa. 42.7–10).

The context in which Isaiah speaks these words, is one of spiritual deliverance for us all. Our captivity is one of sin, our blindness is that to the truth. Isaiah moves into a sublime poetry as he leads us into the light which, eventually, none other than God's own Son will shed. In our darkened state Isaiah sees us as 'a people robbed and spoiled, snared in holes, hid in prison houses, undelivered, spoilt'. He cries, 'Restore!' Christ says, 'I have delivered you, now it is your turn to deliver others. Carry my deliverance into the prison houses, bring out the captives, the hostages to misfortune.'

The news is ever anxious to show us that we live in barbarous times. Yet who can despair when a victim of the prison house can stand up in his 'church', as it were, as did Brian Keenan, and speak such a civilized language? Our duty is to make a bonfire of our easy answers and our platitudes when faced by the camera, and to speak out as an undiminished person.

Brother Benedict and
Sister Scholastica

---◄●►---

I have just been to Hereford to give a talk to the Kilvert
Society on its fiftieth birthday. The Reverend Francis Kilvert, the most intimate and splendid of country parish
diarists. I sat next to Miss Kilvert his cousin who was once
a near-neighbour of mine and, one way and another, I
found myself thinking how close we all become to the
writers we love, never mind when they lived. This was borne
out by a young Benedictine from St Anselm's Abbey, Washington, who was making a pilgrimage, not to an English
shrine, but to the novels of Barbara Pym. Her understanding
of country rectories was not a bit like that of Francis Kilvert
but it was a wonderful understanding all the same. Kilvert
and Pym made a good introduction between myself and
Father Gabriel, for this was the American's name. Having
these authors in common, we felt that we knew each other
pretty well.

But then came St Benedict. How well did I know him?
It is early July and I see his name in the church calendar.
He drew up a Rule for the perfect following of Christ and
became, all unwittingly, the father of Western monasticism.

How frequently this happens in religion. A young man or woman goes off to do their own thing, as we would say, and it turns out to be something which attracts thousands. Very little is known about Benedict himself but it would take an army of historians to give a full account of his achievement. Like John the Baptist, who inspired his way of life, Benedict freed himself from what most of us believe are the necessities of life to enjoy the real freedom of Christ. Crowds of other people were doing it at that time, during the sixth century, going off to deserts and caves and sea-shores but, possibly, getting into some disorder. For Benedict soon realized that if a dozen or so monks were going to set up house together there had to be a Rule, a strict but humane pattern of life. Else all was muddle and discomfort, argument and individualism. And so he wrote the *Rule of Benedict*, and fifteen hundred years later my friend from Washington was still following it. A chapter of Benedict's *Rule* had to be read to the assembled monks each day, which is why the room in which they listened to it is called the chapter house. Our House of Commons first met in the Chapter House of Westminster Abbey – which would have amazed St Benedict, and probably not pleased him. But there it is. Great events are set in motion by some modest rule.

Each of us leaves behind something valuable. It may not be a rule for others to live by, or a book like *The Pilgrim's Progress* to act like a map for the way we should take, but it might well be some indefinable essence of our having been here which mysteriously informs later generations. We occasionally sense this when we come together for a service in a building where worship has taken place for many life-times, a place like the average village church. We sing where others sang, walk where others walked. Nothing dies entirely, nothing, that is, with some good in it. There is a collect which speaks of God preparing for each one of us, 'such good things as pass man's understanding'.

Christ's own rule for those who followed him proved to be too strict for most of them. To forsake all, not even to *prepare* for the journey – no money, no luggage. No looking back. Just walk away – with him. At first, individual Christians did this to the letter, but then came the charismatic teachers like Benedict who found themselves surrounded by followers – as had John the Baptist – and some order had to be imposed. Vows had to be made. Benedict's three vows came to be known as Counsels of Perfection. Those who accepted his Rule would stay poor, stay chaste and be obedient. Their motto would be '*Ora et labora*' – pray and work. The first Benedictines withdrew to a lonely Italian hillside to live by their simple Rule. Over the years their little chapel and its huts became the vast monastery of Monte Cassino whose unimaginable fate was to lie in the path of the Allies' advance during the Second World War and was thus destroyed. Our mighty Benedictine house at Bury St Edmunds lay in the way of the reformers and now it is a municipal garden with flint piles from which the facings have been stripped. It is as though history has sent Benedict's Rule back to its origins. I often sit in roofless

Bury Abbey, smelling the meticulous carpet bedding, watching the children running from cloister to chapter house, from dorter – don't wake the brothers! – to high altar, from the abbots' bridge over the River Lark to the site of Edmund's shrine, and thinking how Benedict himself might have preferred it to its medieval magnificence.

Benedict was not ordained. His was a layman's Rule. He made it with no intention of founding a monastic order. He just lived and died as he thought that the Lord would have wished him to, he and his little band of praying workers. The Rule was austere but not fussy, sensible but not lax. You feel that he wasn't a despot but a young man of intelligence and modesty. A well-balanced person who disliked *dis*order and crazy religious goings on. Once, reading in the outline of the chapter house, I imagined all the Bury monks seated in a huge circle with the Suffolk sunlight pouring through the coloured windows and splashing their black habits with greens and reds and blues, and the odour of dinner wafting from the vast kitchens. It is said that it was a Benedictine monk from Jarrow, Benedict Biscop, who introduced glass windows in English churches, also chants for singing the offices. But the Rule was not set to music. It was plainly said.

Here we sit on St Benedict's Day, the eleventh of July, with the morning sun on us, recollecting some of the many things which spell 'church' for us. We sing Psalm 65 for him, 'Thou, O God, art praised in Sion'. It is customarily a harvest psalm but it is appropriate for a man whose Rule was to reap the greatest of all the monastic harvests, the richest of all the vows of poverty, the most acceptable of all counsels of perfection. A true follower of Benedict's Rule asked little more of life than to work in God's house on earth and to be with Christ when it was done.

I have sometimes thought that verse 7 of our psalm could be saying something about Benedict's sister Scholastica, a library woman by the sound of her. One who said, 'Hush!' The psalm says, 'Who stilleth the raging of the sea, and the noise of his waves, and the madness of the people.'

On St Benedict's day we read of St Paul's organizational ability. He had to make rules for Christians who were leading a communal life. He taught them how to share, how to behave, how to work for the common good. The early Church would have been chaotic without his instructions. We hear about him insisting that the Jewish church in Rome must include Gentiles. He himself shares both Roman and Jewish citizenship. In a Benedictine monastery everything is shared, from talk to silence, from companionship to solitude. As with the Church generally, the simple lives of men and women who lived by simple rules eventually became encased, as it were, in a far from simple architecture. Their vows of poverty were made amidst scenes of artistic splendour and wealth, their prayers said before jewelled shrines. Something which we can no longer comprehend kept the monastic life of the Middle Ages spiritual and profound. Benedict's Rule stays firm amid all the culture and contradictions of history. I note that my Benedictine friend from

Washington DC writes to me on a word-processor, and of course when he comes to England to find Francis Kilvert and Barbara Pym, it is on a plane. The founder of his Order would find no fault in him. As for myself, what a treat it is to be with someone who has accepted counsels of perfection.

The Local Pilgrim

———◆———

S ome years ago I walked the paths of *The Pilgrim's Pro-gress*, being guided along them by an old book by Vera Brittain. Realizing that John Bunyan would have done what he advised others to do, sanctify your own everyday landscape, she used his famous allegory as a map of where he spent all his life as a tradesman, preacher and prisoner. His way to God, his quest for Christ, would be that of the English-speaking world for centuries to come. He came from a long line of yeoman farmers who lived in Elstow, a village on the outskirts of Bedford. He has been mockingly described as a tinker but he was in fact a whitesmith, a skilled artisan who mended pewter and copper utensils. If you go to Bedford museum you can see the heavy anvil which he had to hump along the lanes and which he turned into Christian's heavy load.

It was while Bunyan was working in a mansion at Ampthill that he saw far away the beautiful blue-white ridge of the Chilterns. These became the Celestial Mountains in *The Pilgrim's Progress*, and the mansion itself the House Beautiful. Both would encourage Christian on his journey to Paradise. In Ampthill House he saw works of art and, being himself a craftsman, bellringer and an inspired writer, he recognized that men and women were creative beings and needed music and painting, just as they needed food. Ampt-hill House has long been a shell. The wind and rain pass through its glassless windows and empty door frames. But there, just as Bunyan saw them, are the distant Chilterns saying, 'Make your way to us, we are whole and perfect still.' Bunyan taught us to consecrate the local view, the one which we see all the time. Our Holy Land should not be Palestine or Israel, but where we spend most of our lives. But he also taught us to raise our sights to take in what exists 'above', as it were the supermarket, the motorway, the high street with its banks.

Generations were routed by Bunyan to the City of God. Never before or since has the geography of heaven and earth received such an integration of homeliness and vision, except, of course, in the Gospels themselves, where Christ himself walks through his native fields and breathes his native air. It was the Authorized Version of the Bible, pub-lished in 1611 – only seventeen years before Bunyan was born – which took control of him. He used it to make Bedfordshire the model of an international Puritan quest. *The Pilgrim's Progress* is a prison book and a dream book. Locked up in Bedford Gaol, his charismatic preaching silenced, this sturdy countryman took to the pen. All great prison writing, including that of St Paul, is a way of getting round the frustration of not being allowed to make oneself heard in any other way. They stopped John Bunyan's preaching because in those days only the ordained clergy were allowed the pulpit. During the Commonwealth, 'lecturers', as they were called, often ranted in the parish churches. Some were inspired, all became illegal when King Charles II returned. When they claimed free speech they were told that they could certainly expound what they believed but only if they did so six miles from a city. Thus Bunyan's church – and big congregation – was in the damp Ouse meadows far from Bedford. He was watched and eventually arrested under the Six Mile Act. Would he give his word to stay silent? the magistrate asked. No, he would not. He would preach in the open as his Master had done. And so they took him to Bedford Gaol where, among its horrors, its dirt, its uproar, and fed each day by his blind daughter, he sat at a table and wrote – nearly fifty books!

His masterpiece *The Pilgrim's Progress* was one of the last. It was daring and novel and entirely original. It was written in the language of ordinary people. What would the highly religious public of his day make of it? So nervous was Bunyan of its reception that he wrote a shall-I-publish it, shall-I-not-publish-it poem as its preface. A kind of 'heads I do, tails I don't' piece of wit. His followers were, after all, calling him 'Bishop' Bunyan. And bishops were not supposed to write fancy stuff like this, a story about walking to God.

As did so many followers of Jesus, Bunyan came to him via a spiritual crisis. He described this crisis in *Grace Abounding to the Chief of Sinners*. It is a spiritual autobiography which many literary scholars believe ranks with those of St Augustine and St Teresa. During his late twenties he suffered a severe bout of depression. The dreadful thought came to him that he had committed a sin which was beyond God's forgiveness. Depressive illness can play terrible tricks with our highest belief and with our common sense. Young Bunyan, tall, newly married, wandered through Bedford and saw housewives laughing and chatting on their doorsteps. They would get to heaven and he would not. It was unbearable. He tried to pray but his words made frightening echoes like stones falling down a well. He made a list of his sins. He had played a game called Tipcat on Elstow Green on the Sabbath. He and a wild boy named Harry had gone dancing. But far worse – and wait for it – he was, like thousands of Englishmen at that time, besotted by bellringing. A Cambridgeshire man named Fabian Stedman had published a book on change-ringing and it was sweeping the parishes. Bunyan adored change-ringing but in his religious confusion he convinced himself that God did not, and would let a bell fall on him and kill him. He told puddles to part like the Red Sea as a sign of his faith, and when they did not he told himself that he was no true disciple of the Lord, that he was flawed – worse, that he was damned and would go to hell.

And then one wonderful day his sensible and long-suffering wife (women who marry saints usually have a bad time) found a text which instantaneously destroyed all Bunyan's fears. It was, 'But ye are come unto Mount Sion, and unto the city of the living God . . . and to an innumerable company of angels.' It is the twenty-second verse of Hebrews 12. Bunyan listened, laughed and at once became his old rational, gifted, balanced self. He wrote, 'That night was a good night to me. I never had a better one.' From that moment on he would teach his outdoor congregation, then the English-speaking world how to 'walk with the Lord in the light of the Word' as the old hymn puts it. How to be strong, how never to be afraid whatever happens. How to be glad.

Bunyan is a tough, earthy writer with a prose style which is the literary equivalent of a well-ploughed field. Or a well-made road. The weather blows through it. The Jesus who strode rural Palestine now strides along with those who walk the heavenly highway. On and on walks the Saviour, through villages, towns, past woods and meadows, wells and ponds, along the shore of the great lake, and once in his human exhaustion he envies the foxes and birds their cosy homes. He walks to the wilderness for self-testing and climbs mountains to be near his Father in prayer. He sees wheat, thistles, figs, trees, mustard, brambles, colts, pigs, fish, barns, shepherds, beggars, soldiers, prostitutes, children, disease, beauty, ugliness – the best and the worst of the world. He makes a journey of endless encounters and of withdrawals to silence. He talks as he walks of cleansed men and women journeying through dry places, ever seeking their rest. 'Nevertheless,' he insists, 'I must walk today, and tomorrow, and the day after.' He urges us to 'walk while ye have the light, that ye may be the children of light.

Whither I go ye know, and the way ye know. I am the way.'
His direction is the ultimate direction. 'He that doesn't take
his cross and follow me, is not worthy of me.' Stern stuff.

John Bunyan, now his hero Christian, and his wife Chris-
tiana, walk through Bedfordshire to Paradise. You must do
likewise in Essex or Suffolk, or New South Wales, he tells
us. Walk until the trumpet sounds on the other side. Enjoy
the House Beautiful *en route*, and the blue distance.

During the last week of August 1688 Bunyan rode all the
way from Bedford to London to reconcile a father and son
who had fallen out with each other. It rained all the time.
He caught a chill and died whilst staying with a shopkeeper
friend and was buried in Bunhill Fields. He died on the
fourteenth Sunday after Trinity, the epistle for which says,
'I say then, walk in the Spirit.' One of his books is called
The Heavenly Footman, by which he meant the man who
footed it, as they used to say, all the way home.

Cathedral Camps

Visiting St Paul's Cathedral last Monday I found myself wondering what St Paul would have made of St Paul's. I had forgotten its immensity. The tent-maker, missionary, letter-writer from Tarsus might have lifted his eyes to the great dome and thought, maybe, of the Pantheon in Rome, a new 'cathedral' to all the gods. But it is August in London and a flood of young people from every country in the world, all lightly and brightly clothed, what looked like thousands of them, are taking a rest from their sightseeing on the steps of St Paul's. Queen Anne on her plinth turns her back on them. Pigeons share their lunch. Red buses climb Ludgate Hill. Flags fly. Cameras flash. Voices are in many languages. Also a sense of blessedness existed, I felt. Perhaps it was because the most sought objects of tourism, the pyramids, the Taj Mahal, St Paul's Cathedral, cast a kind of spell on those coming to them for the first time. I too sat on the steps for half an hour or so before entering the familiar church to go about my business, which was to see how the Cathedral Camp was getting on.

More young people from many lands and also on holiday, but now dressed in red T-shirts and wielding dusters and every cleaning device imaginable. They are up ladders, down crypts, balancing on ledges, caught like birds on Tijou's ironwork, hoisted on tombs, flat on tiles, some twenty of them removing the dirt of ages. And I am their Patron and stroll about grandly with their leaders, looking at what they have achieved in a week. Cathedral Camps was the inspiration of Robert Aagaard some twenty years ago, since when most of our cathedrals have been given a unique spring-clean every summer. Experts on the conservation of memorials, glass, wood, or on turning-out ecclesiastical glory-holes, are in charge. I am given tea and tell them that I once climbed the 627 steps to the ball on the top of the dome but they are not awed. I praise their work, enquire about the showers, the food, tell them that it is hot outside, say goodbye, and descend to the crypt.

Old friends here, little Nelson in Cardinal Wolsey's enormous casket, Sir Edwin Landseer for painting Queen Victoria's dogs and making the lions for Trafalgar Square, the gigantic sarcophagus of the Duke of Wellington and, in Painters' Corner, Turner and Reynolds. More tea in the company of most of the generals and admirals of the two world wars, and a lot of German and Japanese boys and girls, all resting their touring feet and eating cake, spreading out street maps and working out what to do next. And so it would be in Notre Dame at this moment, in the cathedrals of St Petersburg, Edinburgh, Sienna, Grafton, New South Wales, where my brother snapped me on the steps to prove that I was there.

Getting about the world is one of the oldest human

activities. Setting foot in some holy place has always seemed a natural thing to do. Our religion is both parish-bound and restless. Some of it is contained on a spot like this for a thousand years, some of it takes us globe-trotting. One could say that it was made on the hoof by those seeking a perfect country which began with the Promised Land and ended with what Jesus called the Kingdom. This morning at Wormingford we have been listening to the tale of a traveller who came to grief. He did not set out to travel very far, just a day's walk from Jerusalem to Jericho, about seventeen miles. Christ told it as an example of disinterested kindness. We have all seen this, particularly when we are far from home. Of someone going out of their way to put a fellow traveller on the right path.

The story of the Good Samaritan would have brought protest from him. 'Good?' Why he was doing what anyone would do in the circumstances. But he would have been wrong. And today there are those who are careful not to get involved, as they describe it. But the more we get about the world, the less easy it is to maintain such an attitude. To pass by some distress which we can easily relieve with very little cost to ourselves. Locked into the Good Samaritan parable are all the pressures of two small nations which hate each other, such as Palestine and Israel, and Northern and Southern Ireland to this day. In the Lord's day Judah and Samaria maintained a despising closeness with each other, unable to do anything else due to their geography and history. Their inheritance flares up on our television screens nightly, lighting up the goodness of the Samaritan story.

It begins memorably. Luke tells it. A lawyer had asked Jesus, 'Who is my neighbour?' and was answered, 'A certain man went down from Jerusalem to Jericho, and fell among thieves, which stripped him of his raiment, and wounded him, and departed, leaving him half dead.' The very economy of these words adds to the horror of what happened. They make us think of the naked, hurt body of the storyteller himself, of his helplessness and plight. Hardly a day passes without a similar assault appearing in our press. It astounds us that an innocent person should be beaten up by a gang either for money, or because he is of another race. The storyteller is geographically correct, and needs to be. His listeners would have known all about that notorious road which descended to Jericho, and some might have retorted, 'More fool him for walking it alone!' How unwise he was. Men travelling from city to city carried money and wore clothes which told their rank. And so the muggers lay in wait in the stony lanes below the Mount of Olives. Jesus doesn't give us the traveller's business, his age or his name. He is just 'a certain man'. What intrigues us about the story is its apparent spontaneity, just that question 'Who is my neighbour?' and it begins. A 'certain lawyer' hears about 'a certain man'. All those who listened to it are being given a glimpse of another journey, that to Christ's kingdom. We are given more than a glimpse of commonplace violence, the kind of thing we all might step around because we see it every day.

The priest has a reason for stepping round the victim. If his clean hands or clean clothes come into contact with blood he will need to be ritually purified before he can do his work. We don't know whether he is going up to Jerusalem or down to Jericho. But whatever, if one gave assistance to every poor wreck one passed on this notorious road, where would one be! Late if nothing worse.

The Levite, that is a man who belonged to the tribe which supplied the Jews with their priests, then arrived on the scene, and his behaviour was worse, because he actually crossed the road to take a look at the poor creature in the gutter. He should have *seen* a fellow human being, a *neighbour*, as Jesus called him. But all he saw was the ordinary misery of life. Some people got there, some came to grief on the way. Hard luck.

'But a certain Samaritan, as he journeyed, came where he was: and when he saw him, he had compassion on him. And he went to him, and bound up his wounds, pouring in oil and wine, and set him on his own beast, and brought him to an inn, and took care of him.' We know that it is Dr Luke retelling the story. The Good Samaritan doesn't even leave the traveller to the mercies of the innkeeper. He stays by his bedside all night, pays the bill, orders the best care of him and should this be more than what he has already given mine host, then he will make it up when he is next that way.

'Now,' says Jesus to someone who believes that he has kept all the requirements of his religion, 'you do likewise.'

Did the Lord go down to Jericho? Yes. He and his disciples were Galileans and so they would often have tramped this old and dangerous road. All down the Jordan valley they travelled, then up to the new Temple on its height. Once, as Jesus was walking from Jericho, blind Bartimeus heard his step and struggled in his darkness to him, throwing away his cloak so as to be able to walk faster and not miss him.

'What do you want?'

'I want my sight back' – So Bartimeus had not always been blind. And then a seeing man walked with Christ the Jericho–Jerusalem road. It was a great moment in the history of travel.

The Good Samaritan is a political as well as a social story. Jesus is teaching that his kingdom is for all, not just for his own countrymen. 'And who is my neighbour?' Well, a Samaritan when he needs help. The Lord's fellow Jews saw them as a religious sect with their own 'temple' and their own version of the law, and disliked them wholeheartedly. And it was uncomfortable to them to hear a story in which their brotherly love outdid that of ordinary Jews. The Samaritan woman at the well is astonished that a Jew like Jesus should speak to her, let alone ask her for a drink. The Church itself has more than once hand-picked its neighbours and not gone out of its way to see Christ in every man or woman, inconvenient though that may be. A collect wants 'to make us love what God commands'. When we do so we hear Jesus saying, 'Blessed are the eyes which see the things which you see.' Blind Bartimeus saw Jesus on the Jericho road. Did tourists travel it in those days? Yes, we know from ancient books that people set out to see the wonders of the world.

The Nine States of Blessedness

It is September, the time of maturity, and we are now advanced enough to understand the ethics of our faith. They are set out in what Matthew calls the Sermon on the Mount, and what Luke calls the Sermon on the Plain. In Matthew's account only the Lord's own hear them, that tiny band of men who had given up their jobs, their home life, their security, their all, to be with him. In Luke's account the world, as it were, listens to the meaning of Christianity. Matthew has the bereaved comforted, Luke has weeping changed to laughter. Both present a thrilling statement of the teachings of Jesus whether from the classic heights or on the ordinary human level.

The mob which besieged Christ wherever he went was naturally keener on cures than on making its way to the kingdom, wherever that was. His disciples were constantly clearing the sick from his path, often forgetting that those who were able to get really close to him could make their own way home unaided. Matthew gives a grim picture of the scene, of 'diseases and torments', of lunacy and palsy, 'of all manner of sickness'. It was from this horrible confusion that Jesus and his circle momentarily escaped to find 'blessedness'. To be blessed means that an individual or a place or an activity becomes the recipient of God's favour. The affluent, the beautiful, the great were disconcerted to hear that they did not necessarily have God's favour. Then who did? And so Jesus begins his long sermon with a list of those who were blessed, even if they did not know it.

Those who realize their need of God are blessed. In fact, the kingdom of heaven is theirs! So just to have a need for God in one's earthly life gives one the key to Christ's realm. No religious qualifications, no sacred discipline, but just this need brings blessing. Then, says Jesus, there is a blessing for sorrow. This blessing is nothing less than the comfort of God himself. There is nothing more difficult than to find words of consolation when someone dies. We fall back on poetry, on texts, on banalities even, and we hear ourselves saying, words, words, words, and we hear the bereaved person forgiving us for saying what she does not need to hear. It will take a little time before she begins to experience God's own consolation. What a blessing it is.

The next beatitude is a shot across the bows of the aggressive, the ambitious, the person whose drive – to mix the metaphor – puts him ahead no matter what the cost to the rest of us. 'Blessed are the meek, for they shall inherit the earth.' In Christ's language meekness is submission to what God would have us do. We are to be courteous, gentle, kind, considerate. In other words, properly civilized. How the old fascists of the last century loathed this beatitude! On its heels comes the blessing for those who are hungry to see what is right prevail. This hunger frequently causes people to be anything but meek, like those who put their lives at risk in destroying wicked leaders, or who sacrifice their own peace for a cause. This is a revolutionary beatitude, a sacrificial beatitude. We bless all those men and women who could not bear to see tyranny, who marched, who spoke out, who frequently died, who made the world better by healing or helping to destroy its wrong politics. People who were greedy for justice, or greedy sometimes for just plain common sense. This uncomfortable beatitude raises a condition before it can be received, which is that one has to be fierce for human rights (and God's rights), and not just someone who says they are a good thing.

Jesus moves on from seeing that right prevails to mercy. This blessing would have rung a bell – that on Aaron's robe – with his followers, who would have recalled a striking passage in Deuteronomy which said, 'When you are in distress you will in days to come turn back to the Lord your God and obey his rules. The Lord your God is merciful: he will never fail you.' Christ then goes on to say that we must not fail each other. And we are reminded of neighbours, friends, fellow workers, some child, our parents even, when they had found themselves in some plight which demanded our mercy. Were we merciful?

And then the Lord comes to that most wonderfully moving of all his beatitudes: 'Blessed are the pure in heart, for they shall see God.' It contains a veiled condemnation of the purity rituals of religion. That priest who would not go near the victim of a mugging on the Jericho road did

The veriest new moon

not do so out of heartlessness but coming into contact with human blood would have made him ritually impure for days to come. Jesus would have none of this. For him it was inward purity alone which mattered. Blessed are the pure in heart, it is *they* who will see God. We, of course, are not here to condemn those who follow other customs in their search for God. The human longing for a vision of God is timeless and intense. As followers of Christ we accept that the way in which we can attain such a sighting of God is to discover the pure heart of our own existence. This is a self-examining beatitude, also a blessing for those who possess what Scripture calls 'innocency'. The seventh beatitude was obvious enough then on the mountainside, and has been plain ever since, although looking at the world since Christ lived in it makes us have every reason to doubt it. 'Blessed are the peacemakers, for they shall be called the children of God.' Peacemakers can be settlers of quarrels between individuals or between nations, or they can be those people who carry a certain peacefulness within them, and who often unconsciously bring a quiet order and a rational kindness with them wherever they go. Often into an unpeaceful house, or workplace. They are 'God's children', says Jesus.

The last two blessings are for the persecuted of every age, men and women who are mocked and abused, or worse, for their faith in Christ – theirs was the kingdom of heaven. Future martyrs would cling to these words. They drenched in suffering, physical and spiritual. It was after giving these blessings to those present and those to come that Jesus told his friends that they were the salt of the earth and the light of the world. 'Let your light so shine before men, that they may see your good works, and glorify your Father which is in heaven' (Matt. 5.16).

It is early September and the Gospel has Jesus walking back from the Mediterranean shore to familiar Galilee, and passing through the Greek-speaking cities of the Decapolis, a journey of many days. On the way he encounters a man who is deaf and who, as with so many people who have never heard, has an impediment in his speech. A thing to be remembered about this story is that it is friends who have placed this man in Christ's way. So this man is loved and cared for. He is not alone. But he cannot hear, he cannot speak properly. All that his friends implore this walking doctor is that 'he puts his hand on him'. But Jesus does something quite extraordinary. He puts his fingers into the deaf ears and his spit on to the tied tongue. This is no ritual gesture but an act of the utmost sharing and intimacy. And he says a commanding, single word – 'Ephphatha!' Be opened! Those who are blessed in the beatitudes may not have much eloquence but they are never tongue-tied. It is a condition of their blessing that they speak out, whether against wrong, or in love. One way or another they are able to show others that God has blessed them.

The Man who Stands at the Gate of Autumn

————◆————

Each season begins with a kind of regret for what has ended. Even the spring. And then we want the spring to be all spring, and the summer all summer. What has autumn to be? Well, John Keats laid down its requirements and we can now hardly think of any that are better. He called autumn 'the bosom-friend of the maturing sun' and that it conspired with this friend in 'loading the vines with fruit' and making apple trees bend from the weight of their crops. He writes about late flowers for the bees and of seeing autumn half-asleep in the half-reaped cornfields, drugged by poppies. And he stoutly defends autumn from all the things we tend to hurl at it, such as its dreariness. He says that it has its own special song and that this includes the song of the gathering swallows as they prepare to leave us for a summer overseas.

Americans call autumn the fall, a word which they most likely took with them when they left Suffolk for Massachusetts. The fall in New England is a sight to be seen. Such woodlands, such colours. Such flaming roads, such turning foliage. It takes one's breath away.

I know people who feel that they must 'fall' at this time of the year, preferably into a soft chair opposite the telly. They complain in clichés. 'We've had the summer – what there was of it! – and now we will mow the lawn for the last time, check the central heating – and flop. We deserve it.' I have always found autumn invigorating. I often begin a new book in the autumn. Autumn suits me. I like its soft light, the smell of its rotting vegetation and what Keats called its 'fruitfulness'. It is a fruitful time for me in every way.

I walked here by the river and saw the banks hanging with berries and heard the rushes rustling. The fish in the clear water swam under drifting leaves. It struck me that it was an excellent season for being alive. Moreover, autumn contains two little summers, St Luke's little summer in October and St Martin's little summer in November. Two benevolent periods when the groaners complain of it being unseasonably warm. As for those dreadful November days in Thomas Hood's poem –

No shade, no shine, no butterflies, no bees,
No fruits, no flowers, no leaves, no birds, November . . .

– the fogs which hid them have all been swept away by the Clean Air Act of the 1950s. Those pea-soupers created in cities by thousands of smoking chimneys also created the atmosphere for Conan Doyle and Dickens but now that they have disappeared by act of Parliament we are able to see autumn clearly, and beautiful it is.

We live by two calendars, one provided by the weather-men and one which we call the liturgy. They don't quite match but they are useful enough. There are many refer-ences to summer and winter in the Bible but none to autumn. And only one to spring. It is to a vine which withers 'in all the leaves of her spring (Ezek. 17.9). Which is what happened to my old russet apple tree this year. In May it was in full flower and leaf, in August it was bare. Trees die. What we have in Scripture is not the four seasons but seedtime and harvest. Jesus applied these two seasons, the growing season and the reaping season, to human exist-ence in many of his sayings and stories. The Bible is an agricultural book where people and creatures of all kinds are fitted into the yearly pattern made by farming and fishing.

Every now and then in the Gospels a figure appears who has nothing to do directly with this pattern and we remember one such today, the first day of autumn. It is Matthew. Who and what was Matthew? Let us take a look at this extraordinary man whose name is fixed to the first Gospel. Is he a man for all seasons like St Thomas More? His symbols are a strange mixture of objects, a sword, a money-bag and a carpenter's square. What kind of person is it who carries with him a sword, a money-bag and a carpenter's square? Scholars say that some of St Matthew's Gospel is borrowed from St Mark's Gospel, and so it cannot be the first Gospel if Mark's had already been written. But our interest is not in this kind of question. It is in the apostle who stands at the gate of autumn and who is described as a 'publican'. I spent my childhood convinced that the good-natured landlords of our local pubs were 'publicans and sinners' and destined for hell. And particularly as my mother was someone who had signed the pledge. Bible language is an interesting hit or miss affair with children. So little was explained to us.

Eventually, of course, I discovered that a publican was a taxman. Matthew collected taxes from his own people for the Romans. This enlightenment did not wholly reprieve Miss Glass who ran the Saracen's Head, for she would separate man and wife, and lover from lover, as they entered her pub, thrusting the men into the bar and the women into her kitchen for a cup of tea. Ladies were never allowed to drink. I imagined her telling herself, 'Well, I may be a publican but I won't be a sinner.'

Matthew's job was the most despised job which a Jew could have. He had bought a permit from the occupying government to collect taxes. How the Jews hated such men. They were traitors. We now know why they were both puzzled and angry when Jesus socialized with 'publicans and sinners'. How could he! Even his excuse did not satisfy them – 'It is the sick who need the doctor.' The company which he kept was scandalous. And it could not have been easy for Peter, Andrew, James and John when Jesus invited Matthew to join their little group. It would have taken some time for their dislike to turn into love.

Matthew is 'called' in chapter 9 of his Gospel. Jesus had been on one of his healing walks before sailing across the

Sea of Galilee to Capurnaum and there, and I quote, 'As he passed from thence he saw a man named Matthew sitting at the receipt of custom, and he said unto him, "Follow me". And he arose and followed him.' No questions. No giving a month's notice to the Romans. No selling his coveted licence to another would-be publican. No regrets. Just, simply, 'he arose and followed him'.

Matthew's Gospel is unlike those of Mark, Luke and John in that it begins with the Lord's family tree, tracing Jesus all the way back to King David. It then gives a full description of how Christ's teaching relates to Jewish law. There is something grand and splendid about the confidence with which it is written. It used to be the most suitable Gospel to be read in church. There is nothing confusing about it. It tells us what Jesus taught, what he did, where he came from and where he *is*. It sets out his law plainly.

Both Matthew himself and his Gospel are wonderful examples of renewal. He comes to us on this first day of autumn with, it could be thought, messages of decline and mortality. But autumn feeds renewal and it will not be long, in the apostle's own words, when we shall be saying, 'A virgin shall be with child, and shall bring forth a son, and they shall call him Emmanuel – God with us.'

Callings and Followings

U ntil recently, when traditional farming methods were overtaken by the machinery and chemicals of the second agricultural revolution, it was easier for us to identify with the fishermen, farmers and shepherds of Scripture than with any other worker in the Bible. The harvest hymns still made sense, the rural year still correctly duplicated the Church's year. But now those engaged in this toil are few and far between, and what was a common sight until just the other day, their seasonal toil, is rare enough for us to stop the car to gaze at it, should we glimpse a cloud of gulls following a ploughman, or lambing in springtime.

Curiously, the worker in Scripture whose modern counterpart is an increasingly familiar figure to us is the 'publican'. The publican of the Gospels is the taxman, someone who was even less popular then than he is now. The Jews themselves had levied a Temple tax ever since the reign of King David, and that during the Lord's day was bad enough. But when the Roman occupation arrived and a second tax to support the empire was added to the Temple tax, well we can imagine the anger. Worse, the Romans licensed local men to collect their tax because these would know all about the local economy. These licences had to be purchased. Those who paid for them and used them to collect money for Rome were called 'publicans'. Levi, soon to be Matthew, was a publican, a man who collected taxes from his own race for the occupying power. The scandalous nature of his calling apart, Matthew would have been what we would describe as a 'professional'. It makes us recall what some of the other disciples of Jesus were, those who were not so-called humble fishermen. Luke was a doctor, and some say an artist. Certainly, like Mark, he was a great writer. Judes not only looked after the funds of the Twelve and their Master, but had some kind of access to the Temple treasures. We might call him a banker. Jesus himself was, of course, 'the carpenter's son' from workaday Nazareth. So here at the very beginning of the Church we have businessmen, craftsmen and agriculturalists, and maybe poets and artists, coming together to promote its teachings, each one of them pointing the way to Christ's kingdom.

Matthew's Gospel is thought to be the oldest of the four and it lays stress on Christ's 'new law' and it gives his teachings in full. It must have been a total transformation for an ex-tax-collector to have to write down Jesus's indifference to money – to his putting money in its place, which was to him a long way down the list of what we should want, should strive to have. As a publican Matthew would have endured much abuse, hatred even. We ritually hate the taxman whilst knowing full well that we cannot have our roads, schools, defence, medicine – practically everything necessary to us as a nation – did he not gather their

Cow crossing a narrow bridge

cost from us. Modern politics, by whatever party, is really the art of government by 'publicans' in chief. We grouse but we pay up. What we ultimately demand of government is a wise, even an inspired, use of the funds it takes from us.

Matthew's, or Levi's seat of custom was in Capernaum, a Roman garrison town which became Jesus's headquarters after he had been run out of Nazareth. It was the scene of many of the wonderful things which he did and many of the wonderful words which he spoke. Who could go on collecting taxes after seeing and hearing such things! Matthew's calling can hardly surprise us. There was a rational element in his character. Perhaps, like us, he had thought it obvious that good roads, even if they were Roman roads, had to be paid for, and now he thought it obvious that someone who spoke and acted as this extraordinary teacher did should be listened to. He found the new law not only exciting but intelligent. He makes an unattractive figure in medieval art when compared with the fishermen disciples, clasping as he does two fat money-bags. The New Testament lumps publicans and sinners together, but we have no record of Matthew being corrupt. He was simply a professional man at the seat of custom – custom and excise. In the eyes of the Jews it was a very different matter, one of collaboration with the enemy. But then Jesus 'called' him. He heard that irresistible invitation, 'Follow me'. No longer would Matthew be seated, but walking. And so he closed down the office and opened up a marvellous new movement in his life. He wrote a line under his transactions and began a book – the Gospel according to Matthew.

Matthew comes to us in the most businesslike week in the old farming year, that preceding Michaelmas, when tithes were paid to the Church and harvest profits were totted up, when labourers changed masters and tides changed with the equinox. The summer past, men followed work wherever it happened to be. We still talk of some guru having 'a following'. We follow all kinds of teachings, some of them we know not to be serious though they attract us at the time. There were thousands of men and women – and children – who abandoned their humdrum tasks or play to follow the itinerant Jesus in the physical sense. On and on over the Palestinian countryside they roamed in his magical wake, enthralled by his stories and awed by his healing power. Now and then he would make his escape from their clamour, slipping away to some lonely spot or boarding a little boat and sailing out of their reach.

It took the followers of Christ some while to learn that they must follow him in their trades and professions, in their homes and in their leisure – at a party, for example. We hear of the brothers James and John slipping back to Lake Galilee now and then to do a day's fishing or mending of nets. One of the most sublimely everyday 'asides', as it were, in the Gospels is when we hear, after his being commissioned an apostle, that Peter goes fishing. But we have no news of Matthew returning to the tax office at Capernaum to count up the figures. In a world of endless financial talk we are closer to Matthew than to any of the other disciples. He intrigues us, even if we do not go as far as calling the Inland Revenue the haunt of publicans and sinners. He was called to something mightier than bureaucracy, something compelling but yet, as that moment of calling, something which must have seemed to him vague and inefficient. Yet he must go! And so he closed the office and opened for himself a path to God which he would like us to tread as well.

Many things in Scripture are remote to us, but not this word 'calling'. For some are still called to the colours or to the bar. It implies some mysterious voice which enchants us to take up a way of life which has within it something more than the actual duties and skills of a particular job. St Paul often became worried about the Lorelei-like calling of false prophets. Religious preachers and teachers can be so seductive, particularly when they are wrong but not evil. How were those who were waiting and praying for a 'call' to know when it was the right one? When God called Samuel he thought it was his teacher old Eli, and when the call came for the third time the poor priest had to face up to the terrible fact that such a call would never be for him. Jesus was bleak. 'Many are called but few are chosen.' I suppose he meant that many think that they are called when they are not. On the other hand we have all met people who do their best to live up to what they sincerely believe to be their calling, uncertain though they may be.

St Paul took a liberal view of being called. 'As the Lord

hath called every man, so let him be. Let every man abide in the same calling wherein he was called' (1 Cor. 7.20). This advice used to be the basis of the old social policy of people keeping to their station in life, ignoring as it does the thrilling statement that it is Christ who calls each and everyone of us at some time, and in some way or other. Calling us, like Matthew, from the seat of custom.

The Angels Keep their
Ancient Places

————◄◉►————

A nd so we come to the glitteringly named Feast of
St Michael and All Angels, or in the plain talk of
farmers, Quarter Day. *The* Quarter Day when not all that
long ago men changed masters, farms changed hands, rents
were paid and the parson received his tenth. Harvest was
in, or should be, preparation was made for the cold days
ahead, leaves turned, cottages were thatched and patched,
fruit was picked and where agriculture was concerned the
year had come to an end. And high above this workaday
business was this supernatural host of angels and archangels,
this blissful choir, this winged protection. Who and what
were they? Artists and poets gave one answer, the Church
another. Country folk mixed these answers together and
added their own. Angel comes from the Greek for messenger. Who sends the messenger? God.

The gods of Mount Olympus sent Mercury. We go to
the Mercury Theatre just up the road in Colchester, and
there he is, just about to take off from the roof on his
winged feet, a charming copy of a Roman statue which was
discovered in a temple at Sheepen Farm nearby. Travellers

to Colchester would have prayed to him, using him like a mobile phone to put into some merchant's ear that they were on their way with excellent business for both of them. Like angels, Mercury was kind enough to carry both divine and humdrum messages.

In the Old Testament we read of Jacob wrestling with an angel all night and the angel eventually overcoming him. Sculptors have been drawn to this combat. But what was really happening? It was Jacob wrestling with God's message for him. In Genesis creation is attended by an innumerable multitude of angels, or messages from the Creator. Job puts these messages to music, being a great poet. His angels sing and play instruments. Throughout Scripture angels mediate between God and humanity. And still winged instruction, winged care comes to us all our days. Francis Thompson was so enthralled by this that he believed it was not beyond any of us to catch both the message and a fleeting glimpse of the messenger:

> The angels keep their ancient places;
> Turn but a stone, and start a wing!
> 'Tis ye, 'tis your estrangèd faces,
> That miss the many-splendoured thing.

When we come to Jesus we find that there are angels present throughout his life. They 'minister' to him, a wonderful word. Their duty is to see to his needs. They are present at his birth, and present when he is in greatest need of his Father's advice, in the wilderness and in the Garden of Gethsemane, where the terrible message is that he must die if we – humankind – are to live. Angels may be a part of a religious imagination which is now beyond our comprehension but when we read how real they were to Jesus they become actual to us, although not in the medieval sense. Strangely, art has obscured their meaning. How physical they are in the church windows and in the church roof, such faces, such pinions, such ravishing clothes. Archangels, angels, cherubim, seraphs all crowded together to form the heavenly power or choir or court. But back in the Gospels they go about God's business, and back in our own personal experience we remember how God prompted us in what to do, where to go, how to act. His message came through during some crisis in our affairs and we felt the brush of an angel's wing. It was angels, not men or women, who were the first witnesses of the resurrection. It seemed as if they were acting in reverse that Easter morning, carrying the message from Joseph of Arimathea's briefly occupied tomb back to God as well as declaring it to the world.

Jesus once spoke quite shockingly about our impossibility of escape from certain messages which angels carried from earth to heaven. He had just finished telling his followers how they had to become like children in order to enter his kingdom, when he drew a boy to him to demonstrate that each child possessed a personal angel who would carry report of any harm done to him back to God. Here is a picture of the guardian angel. One of the earliest prayers taught to children says, 'May angels guard us while we sleep, till morning light appears'.

So what of angels in art, glass angels, carved angels, the angel voices in our hymns, the stony angels in the cemeteries, the angels of the poets? What of the Archangel Michael himself who had fought a war in heaven and defeated the dark angel Satan? They are, rather like our winged Mercury, inspired artefacts which show us better than anything else the two-way communication between men and women and their Creator. Our guardian angels are not packed away with our toys. They are with us until we are with God. Sometimes their winged protection joins God's winged protection, as in the ninety-first psalm – 'He shall defend thee under his wings, and thou shalt be safe under his feathers ... For he shall give his angels charge over thee, to keep thee in all thy ways.'

Frequently when we are quiet, maybe in church when there is nothing going on, perhaps when walking home, perhaps when lying wide awake in bed to listen to the wind rushing through the trees, we hear quite clearly being inwardly told what to do, where to go, when to speak. Or a voice which tells us, 'Rest now, for I am with you always.' The angel speaks.

The other day I had to guide the newly constituted Robert Bloomfield Society around the poet's countryside, which is that stretch of light, rather sandy country which runs from Bury St Edmunds to Thetford, and which was until a century or so ago East Anglia's moor. Only now it is partly ploughed and partly aforested. Bloomfield was born in Honington and in the year 1800 he published a famous rural poem, *The Farmer's Boy* which he wrote while in exile in London and working as a shoemaker in a leathery kind of sweatshop. It sold a fabulous 26,000 copies but it did not make him rich. Indeed, so poverty-stricken was he towards the end of his life that he turned his hand to making and selling wind harps. They were called Aeolian harps after Aeolus the god of the winds. Bloomfield made exquisite wind harps, being a great craftsman, and people bought them and fixed them in their windows so that the wind could 'play' them. King David woke one night to hear his harp being played, presumably by a breeze since there was nobody in the room except himself. And Elgar listened to the wind harp in his window whilst he was working on his violin concerto. He told a friend, 'The sound of a distant Aeolean harp flutters under and over the solo.' As a child I was mysteriously enchanted by the wind in the telegraph wires and the sound of the sea in some large shells which came from India, the fall and rush of waves on an unknown shore.

Thus composers pluck music from the air and writers their dream territories from captivating noises. Those who follow Christ 'hear him' in silence as well as in the sounds we make in church. We hear his angel while we are washing up or mowing the lawn, or parking the car. Whether we are at the altar or in the supermarket, the protective wings are felt by us and we know that we are included in the music around the Throne. It is a satisfying thought.

The Lay Voice

The Book of Amos is a *tour de force*, confidently written, poetic, dramatic and with a happy ending. But its author, who sounds young, apologizes for having written it. 'I am not a prophet, nor am I the son of a prophet. I am only a farmer from Tekoa who looks after animals and an orchard.' Well, I always tell myself after reading him, 'Tell that to the marines – or their sceptical equivalent in his day.' Of course, what Amos is insisting on, to both us and his contemporaries, is that although indeed he lacked official permission to say what he did, he had to speak out. Such an urge has its legitimacy at all times. State or Church, or a combination of both, do nothing or do wrong, and a so-called ordinary man or woman cannot stay silent.

Amos lived during the reign of King Uzziah some 750 years before Christ. Whilst acknowledging Uzziah's authority, Amos said that God had taken him out of the king's flock. In other words, he had disenfranchised himself in order to have a free voice. A disaster was brewing and somebody had to say so. But a warning from a young farmer? Who was going to take any notice of that? And Tekoa? Has anyone heard of Tekoa? If Judah had to be warned, let the warning come from the proper place, Jerusalem.

But Amos's simple life and work, so different and distant from that of the capital, had given him a perspective. He could see what those on top of things could not see. And so he raised his voice. Judah was in no mood to listen to it. Blessed with many years of peace and prosperity, pleasantly ruled by an amiable monarch, it was on what we would call a high. It grew richer by the year and had become delightfully civilized. Gone all that shepherding and gone all that primitive thanks for its existence. As always, of course, only a fraction of the people were benefiting from all this prosperity and little of it reached the nation at large. Justice was slack. The poor were pushed around as usual. In the Temple glorious singing and ceremonies went on all day long. Amos could see what must happen – and that very soon. God would step in to say, 'I am more than beautiful liturgy.' And there was another matter which was upsetting the priests. This impertinent and untrained prophet in Tekoa was daring to tell the world that God was not only the God of Judah but the God of all nations, a God who revealed himself in human history, no matter where or when. It was true that he had a special relationship with his chosen people because it was they who had first recognized him as the only God, but he was still the God of mankind.

Further than this, Amos was uncomfortably reminding Judah that the famous covenant which existed between God and it was rooted in righteousness. This meant that 'the day of the Lord' to which Judah looked forward with such longing, and which they saw as a golden age, would be – must be – a day of justice as well. And so, if Judah went on as it did at present, 'the day of the Lord' would be a black day indeed. A day of punishment. It was disgraceful that they had to listen to such statements as, 'The Lord will roar from Zion, and utter his voice from Jerusalem, and the habitations of the shepherds shall mourn, and the top of Carmel shall wither.'

One of the gifts which God gives to those who speak his truth is a remarkable language. Herdsman, orchardman, Amos might be but he had a great voice. It brought astonishment as well as anger to those who heard him. His brief book comes towards the end of the Old Testament and it is a wonderful read. It opens with a dire list of fates for the various erring tribes and cities, reminding them of the culture and heritage which God gave them – everything which made life worth living. And which, alas, they were now either taking for granted or totally forgetting. Ignoring would be a better word. He tells them that luxury will not be able to protect them – that it means nothing to God.

And I will smite the winter house with the summer house, and the houses of ivory shall perish, and the great houses have an end. (Amos 3.15)

Nor will all those beautiful services in the Temple placate God, who is furious with them. 'Take them away from me the noise of thy songs, for I will not hear the melody of thy viols. I hate, I despise your feast days. I will not smell the incense of your solemn assemblies!'

This was too much and the high priest of Bethel told Amos to go where they couldn't hear him, and prophesy there! It was outrageous of him to criticize both Church and state as he did. He reminded him that Uzziah was in charge. 'Prophesy not again at Beth-el, for it is the King's chapel and the King's court.' Amos was trespassing.

It is then that we have Amos's apologia. 'I was no prophet, neither was I a prophet's son. I was a herdsman and a gatherer of sycamore fruit. But the Lord took me as I followed the flock and told me, "Go, prophesy unto my people Israel."' He adds, 'God showed me a basket of summer fruit and said, "Amos, what do you see?" And I said, "A basket of summer fruit." And God said, "The end is come upon my people of Israel."' We hear the sadness in his voice.

Summer fruit ends the growing year. It was while I was picking up my enormous 'harden' pears yesterday afternoon – they are actually too high to reach and I have to wait until the first autumn gales bring them down – that I thought of Amos and his God in the sycamore fig orchard. The wind, wild and passionate, was like his voice and it brought me to him. Every now and then great civilizations begin to crumble all unknowingly, someone speaks an unpalatable truth – says what has to be done in an unforgettable language. Says it from the housetops, says it from the prison. And those in power say, 'Who gave *him* leave to speak?'

God told his unofficial prophet Amos, 'I will send a famine in the land, not a famine of bread, but of my words.' But neither God nor prophet can bear to starve their people to death and Amos's book ends with the promise of rebuilt cities and a replanted countryside, and a repentent nation. It may be the story of a tiny state ages ago but it continues to be the story of many lands today.

Doctor Luke

———⟨◈⟩———

We are in St Luke's little summer. The late October sun fires the village. It is warm enough to eat outside. The Roman bricks which make such fine corners for the tower are hot to the touch. There is the mere hint of thinning foliage. The hedges are gaudy, the grass is wet gold. The old farmers would have said, 'If it comes to the worst, we can get the harvest in on St Luke's.' it is quite usual in East Anglia for Luke's summer to last a fortnight or more.

One of the things which has always intrigued me when reading Luke is that he addresses both his books, his Gospel and the Acts of the Apostles, not to the world at large but to a man named Theophilus. Who is this 'most excellent Theophilus'? To me he sounds like a publisher, for Luke wrote for everyone and not for a single individual, and when these wonderful books arrived at Theophilus's house, it was clear that they were not intended for a private library, but for distribution. Luke would have known that his friend would have made them public knowledge. They are, he tells him, eyewitness accounts of what happened when and after Christ was on earth which he, Luke, has put together to certify what occurred. They are a great read. Acts alone is one of the best travel books ever written. I imagine Theophilus unrolling these scrolls and asking himself, 'What can this extraordinary person not do?' Doctor, artist, now author – and evangelist too, of course!

Theologians believe that Luke was a Gentile convert to Christianity who spoke and wrote Greek. Not the elegant Greek of the learned, but the Greek which one would hear in the market place. He accompanied St Paul on the second and third of his missionary journeys, ending up in Rome with him, and he was at Antioch where the gospel was first proclaimed in Europe. He was unmarried, wrote his Gospel in Greece and died aged eighty-four. It is thought that he may have been one of the frightened followers of Christ who were walking to Emmaus after the crucifixion. His biography is both finely detailed and open to suggestion. We need a wholly non-mythical, non-legendary Luke and in every important sense we have one. For us he is that rounded man, a good doctor and a 'physician of the soul'. The essence of Luke's books is that Christ is for the world, and not just for the Jews. His world is the Roman Empire and his Church is as full of capable women as capable men. He names them. He also gives a greater prominence to prayer than the three other Gospel writers. Luke fits into today's Christianity with a certain twenty-first-century ease. He does not perplex us as much as do some of the New Testament figures. It is our devotion to medicine which causes Luke to be particularly acceptable at this moment. We can trust Dr Luke. We agree with what he says and like what he was. There is an understanding between us which is unique in religion.

Was it not to men and women with Luke's qualifications that Jesus's command to evangelize would have an historic appeal? 'The harvest is truly great, but the labourers are few.' Go out to work in what is still called the mission field. Until recently the mission field was in Africa or China, now it is in this country. Those we taught are now teaching us. Luke would not have found this ironic. He loved the rationality of Christ, his clear-headedness, when for instance, criticized for the company he kept, the Lord retorted, 'It is not the healthy who need a doctor, but the sick. I have not come to invite the virtuous to my table, but the repentant sinner.'

The miracles in St Luke's Gospel reflect his special understanding of human nature, of its suffering and its complexity. It is the understanding which is part scientific and part that of the writer-artist. Christ's own ministry of healing of mind and body was non-stop. Luke watched and learned from it. His medical training had taught him much about the flesh and the psyche, and about the stoicism or terror of those in pain or despair. And so his happiness knows no bounds when Christ makes life worth living again for some ill person, or returns life to some young victim who has died too soon. We have no account in the New Testament of Jesus raising the old from death. They have had their full span. It is Luke who writes about the widow of Nain. There she is, poor woman, burying her son, when the Lord of life stops the funeral as it winds its sad way through the town gate, touches the bier and then – the thrillingly happy return to their home. Dr Luke would have so often broken the news of a boy's or girl's death to their parents. It would have been all part of his day's work. But then, too, there would have been the days when, due to his skill, the temperature went down and the child sat up, and those who had sent for him felt like kissing his feet.

Civilization has always placed wisdom at the forefront of what is most required in rulers. Luke, the beloved physician as Paul called him, was wise above all things. It may be hard for us to see what Jesus first saw in those he chose to be his apostles, but we can certainly see why Luke was among them. He was both imaginative and sensible. It is Luke who always picks up the Lord's medical references. There is the woman bent double who is made upright, the man cured of dropsy – on the Sabbath of all days – that group of lepers, ten in all but only one not too frantic with joy at being cured who said thank you. Children can behave like this when they are given their heart's desire. In all his reference to healing Luke is clearly moved by the kindness of Christ. Signing off his letter to the Colossians, Paul sends 'greetings from our dear friend Luke the doctor'.

But what of Luke 'the physician of the soul'? The soul is the name for what survives of each one of us after physical death. It can be hurt, it can be corrupted. It can be blackened. In religious language Jesu is the lover of my soul, Dr Luke its physician, and via them, 'all the diseases of our souls may be healed'. Today's medicine deals with body and spirit. Physical illness can come from spiritual unhappiness.

Christ's ministry, and copied by his friends, seeks wholeness of mind and flesh. There is an old hymn which says:

> Saviour, of thy bounty send
>   Such as Luke of Gospel story,
> Friends to all in body's prison,
>   Till these sufferers see thy glory.

St Luke's little summer brings soft winds, bright colours, the last scents of summer proper, and a whiff of decay.

'And they found him in
the Temple'

To celebrate someone or something means to honour
him or it with ceremonies and festivities. We celebrate
birthdays, Christmas and Holy Communion. We celebrate
a monarch's jubilee and saints' days. We celebrate comings
of age, marriages – but not funerals. Although in some
societies, and at one time in Christian society, the day when
the spirit was freed from the flesh and returned to God *was*
a festal day. White was worn. Hymns of joy were sung.

The word 'celebrate' appears only three times in the
Authorized Version of the Bible, once in Leviticus, when
God gives his people the list of feasts which they are to
observe and tells them, 'from even unto even shall ye celebrate your sabbath', which they continue to do to this day.
And again in Leviticus, the book of the priesthood, when
God inaugurates the Feast of Tabernacles and says that it
is to be celebrated in the seventh month of the year; and
then in Isaiah, when King Hezekiah is dying, too young, he

thinks, and asks God to give him fifteen more years. The poor sick king petitions for this longer life in a beautiful song in which he reminds God that 'death cannot celebrate thee'. I am too young to die – 'I am deprived of the residue of my years.' Hardly a day passes when in wars and accidents and illness we do not read about those who are deprived of the residue of their years. King Hezekiah's petition succeeded. But, alas, he lived to see himself and all his subjects taken captive.

Walking the Malvern Hills, I suddenly remembered a fascinating celebration which took place just below me a few years ago when the Archbishops of Canterbury and York came here to give thanks for the life of their predecessor William Temple. Here was a man who might well have asked God for fifteen more years, for having been enthroned in 1942, he was to die in 1944. The whole country was appalled and the Church itself was stunned. William Temple's death is still regarded as a loss which nothing has been able to heal. But why come to Malvern to celebrate that brief ministry? The answer is a story which goes back many centuries and which the lovely landscape itself partly relates. For I was wandering through the scenes of some of the finest Christian poetry and music – could almost hear it on the wind. William Temple came here to listen to it when Christian civilization stood on the brink of the abyss, when Fascism was sweeping across the world.

But first, who was William Temple? And why when he did not live long enough to put his undoubtedly inspired plans into action does he continue to inspire us? Three short wartime years were all that were given him and yet he changed the Church's thinking, and continues to do so still. One has only to say his name and the gossip and clerical trivia disappear. We are serious and intelligent once again, and full of love and respect for the often much trivialized Church of England. William Temple. Born in 1881 in a Victorian bishop's palace, the son of a future Archbishop of Canterbury, he was among those who laid the foundation of today's social Christianity. He spoke with a kind of intellectual simplicity which dismissed the various class languages which dominated religion during the first half of the twentieth century. He destroyed almost single-handedly – or single-voicedly – the fustian of the Church. He helped Rab Butler with his great 1944 Education Act and put his influence behind the Workers' Educational Association, a movement which gave thousands of intelligent men and women an entrée, as it were, to their own national literature and art, philosophy and science. He and men like Bishop Bell of Chichester, stood out against, not only Nazism, but some of the methods which were being used to fight it.

When he was twenty-five William Temple decided to be ordained but was turned down by the Bishop of Oxford as 'unsafe' where some of his beliefs were concerned. Many of the saints were 'unsafe'. Christ's often-repeated instructions to his friends were to strike out in unconventional religious directions. Shortly after his eventual ordination,

William Temple went to live in Australia and tour the universities there. The First World War found him joining Dick Sheppard to free the Church of some of its state shackles. During the 1920s Westminster Abbey would be crowded when it was known that he was preaching there. In 1929 he became Archbishop of York and from then onwards he became a thrilling voice which revitalized the Church. George Bernard Shaw, an agnostic, declared that to have an Archbishop like William Temple was 'a realized impossibility'.

And so why did he decide to hold a conference at Malvern in 1941 when the world was falling apart and Hitler looked as though he would reign over its moral ruins? It was a hot August and Temple drew the Church leaders there to see how the Church could best present a social gospel. He was sixty and had seen the poverty and squalor which existed in Britain, the then richest country in the world, and the one which exported its Christianity to a vast empire. What a time for such a debate – and what a curious setting to hold it in.

It was because a revolutionary poem had been set there, *Piers Plowman*, in the fourteenth century when the Black Death had pretty well destroyed the structure of the state. William Langland the author was telling the England in which a third of the population had died, never mind the Christ of cathedrals, wealthy abbeys, lords and prelates. Let the nation come to a field below the Malvern Hills and find him as a Plowman and the place to worship him, a barn.

William Langland had been born near this field, the son of a woman farmer. A later writer, another local boy, was at that time the Poet Laureate, John Masefield. And the Malverns too were the home hills of Edward Elgar whose great works were at that moment being shamefully neglected. So here was an Archbishop of Canterbury convening a meeting of the Church of England during the worst days of the Second World War on a spot immortalized in poetry and music. *Piers Plowman* called a country to its senses – you might say its common senses.

Every now and then in our history someone comes along and pulls us out of a rut – often a religious rut. During that wartime summer a new Archbishop took a visionary look at Christianity where the poet William Langland had taken his visionary stare at it, where he had repudiated its materialism and unfairness and where, in the guise of an ordinary man, he had watched Christ at work in the fields, one who grew the food for his fellows. For an all too brief while William Temple fed the English soul with the Bread of Life. I sat on the top of the Herefordshire Beacon, thinking about him and about *The Dream of Gerontius*, Elgar's setting of an old priest's vision of his own death and immortality, and realizing that one does not necessarily have to live a long time to change the world for the better.

Containers

———◆———

The most common find in archaeology is pottery. Scraps of broken pottery, perfect pots, pots of all ages, some glazed, some decorated, some plain clay. But all utilitarian, if only to put a rose in. Civilizations depended, not on rulers, armies and priests, but on pots. Wine pots, food pots, cooking pots, pots for human ashes, and all made of clay. Clay shaped on a wheel then baked in a kiln. There were pots which went once too often to the well and got broken, and pots which, though essentially the same, tell us that they came from China or Mexico or Gaul or Egypt, vast numbers of them and, considering their age, miraculously whole. I often gaze at the Roman and Saxon pots in Colchester Castle. There they sit just waiting for a hare to be jugged in them, some a thousand, some two thousand years old, and without so much as a chip or a crack. And for most of their time buried deep in the earth. And yet the earth had not reclaimed the potter's clay but held it in its shape, and often not so much as staining it, so that when the archaeologists dug it up it was as good as new.

The one essential object in a house of any period was a pot. Those water jars at Cana were clay pots. To see a potter at work is mesmerizing. Brenda leaves her pottery, to sing in the choir. We have watched her foot spinning the wheel, the shining clay rising between her wet hands, and what was simply a lump becoming the most classic of all shapes, a vase. Some potters are included among the world's great artists, Bernard Palissy and Bernard Leach. Pots have a base and a lip and a generous swelling between them. To watch pots coming into shape is one of the world's therapeutic activities. It soothes, it inspires, it looks so easy. But it is enormously skilled. How we all long to do it, to spin the potter's wheel! To feel the potter's clay!

The potter is the top artisan in Scripture. Which is hardly surprising, for every character in the Bible would have watched him. He was the person who most closely resembled his Maker. God made him out of clay and he deals with the same basic material, fashioning it, raising it up, firing it. When his people disobey him, God tells Jeremiah to break a pot before them as an illustration of what will happen to Jerusalem if they do not mend their ways. 'Thus saith the Lord of hosts; Even so will I break this people and this city, as one breaketh a potter's vessel, and it cannot be made whole again!'

Poor Job, perhaps more than anyone else in the Old Testament, recognized our human fragility. He never forgets his origins. 'I am formed out of the clay.' Jeremiah is equally humble and tells each one of us that 'we are in God's hands, as clay in the potter's hand'. In creating us God is not making something which is merely functional, he is moulding our clay in his own image. Isaiah was overwhelmed by this and says wonderingly, 'We are clay, *thou* art the potter.' Potters were such an important part of Israel's economy that they are listed by name in Chronicles. 'These were the potters and those that dwelt among plants and hedges.' This reference to where the pots were made always reminds me of the Suffolk claypits where we played as children. Exciting sunken watery beds where the brickmakers dug their 'pug' for the mill, and which in early spring were bordered with clay-loving plants such as coltsfoot. Those 'hedges' mentioned in Scripture would have been the banks round the potter's claypit.

Jesus made clay on one memorable occasion. It was as if he was remembering his Father's use of it. He gathered a handful of road-dust and moistened it with his saliva, turning it into a little poultice for a blind man's eyes. It is one of those unforgettable acts of his special tenderness, like that when he inserted his fingers in deaf ears, or touched a leper. St Francis imitated the touch of Christ by kissing a leper and his mouth on that loathed flesh did in its own way re-mould it.

Re-moulding ourselves has always been a human longing. Omyá Kháyyám the Persian poet puts this longing into words:

> Ah Love! Could thou and I with Him conspire
> To grasp this Sorry scheme of Things entire,
> Would not we shatter it to bits - and then
> Re-mould it nearer to the Heart's Desire!

The poet thinks of God's love for what he has made:

> And He that with his hand the Vessel made
> Will surely not in after Wrath destroy.

He remembers those who are born with mental or physical defects.

> After a momentary silence spake
> Some Vessel of a more ungainly make;
> 'They sneer at me for leaning all awry:
> What! did the Hand then of the Potter shake?' . . .
> Who is the Potter pray, and who the Pot?

God's creation goes beyond its basic materials. A pot may be made of clay but it becomes more than clay. It will be beautiful because it is useful, beautiful because it is a work of art, or sometimes beautiful because it is both. What raises it from common clay is the potter's hand. What raises us from the dust is the hand of God. He sees us as individual vessels which have to be filled with his Spirit. When we die, our earthen part returns naturally to the earth and our spiritual part returns to God. Which is what heaven means.

ACKNOWLEDGEMENTS AND BIBLIOGRAPHY

Bell, Adrian, *Men and the Fields*, illustrated by John Nash, Batsford, 1938.

Bible, Authorized Version and New English.

Bonhoeffer, Dietrich, *Letters and Papers from Prison*, third revised and enlarged edition, SCM Press, 1967.

Book of Common Prayer.

The Cloud of Unknowing and Other Works, Penguin Books, 1972, new translation by A. C. Spearing, 2001.

Dickinson, Emily, *The Complete Poems*, edited by Thomas H. Johnson, Faber & Faber, 1970.

Eliot, T. S., 'The Journey of the Magi', *Selected Poems*, Faber & Faber, 1954.

Hymns Ancient and Modern, Canterbury Press Norwich, 1922, 1950 and 1983.

Keenan, Brian, *An Evil Cradling*, Hutchinson, 1992.

New English Hymnal, Canterbury Press Norwich, 1986.

The Rubaiyat of Omár Kháyyám, translated by Edward Fitzgerald.

The Rule of St Benedict, translated by David Parry OSB, Gracewing, 1990.

Saint John of the Cross, *Poems*, translated by Roy Campbell, Harvill Press, 1952.

Thompson, Francis, 'The Kingdom of God – In No Strange Land' in *The Oxford Book of English Verse 1250–1918*, Oxford University Press, second edition 1939.

Traherne, Thomas, *Centuries*, edited by Anne Ridler, Oxford University Press. 1966.